bäco

bäco

Vivid recipes from the heart of Los Angeles

Josef Centeno
and Betty Hallock

photographs by **Dylan James Ho and Jeni Afuso**

CHRONICLE BOOKS
SAN FRANCISCO

Names: Centeno, Josef, author. | Hallock, Betty, author.
Title: Bäco : vivid recipes from the heart of Los Angeles / by Josef Centeno
    and Betty Hallock ; photographs by Dylan + Jeni.
Description: San Francisco : Chronicle Books, [2017]
Identifiers: LCCN 2016057668 | ISBN 9781452154688 (hc : alk. paper)
Subjects: LCSH: Cooking. | LCGFT: Cookbooks.
Classification: LCC TX714 .C4465 2017 | DDC 641.5—dc23 LC record
available at https://lccn.loc.gov/2016057668

Manufactured in China.

MIX
Paper from
responsible sources
FSC www.fsc.org   **FSC™ C008047**

Prop styling by Betty Hallock
Food styling by Josef Centeno and Andy Villaluna
Designed by Vanessa Dina
Typesetting by Frank Brayton

10 9 8 7 6 5 4 3 2 1

Chronicle books and gifts are available at special quantity discounts to
corporations, professional associations, literacy programs, and other
organizations. For details and discount information, please contact our
premiums department at corporatesales@chroniclebooks.com or at
1-800-759-0190.

Chronicle Books LLC
680 Second Street
San Francisco, California 94107
www.chroniclebooks.com

AUTHORS' ACKNOWLEDGMENTS

This book is part love letter to downtown Los Angeles. Thank you to all of the neighbors, friends, and customers whom we have met here over the years.

Thank you to the staff at Bäco Mercat, Bar Amá, Orsa & Winston, Ledlow, and P.Y.T. You are the pulse of the corner at Fourth and Main streets. Many had a direct hand in making this book—by pitching in to test, tweak, measure, re-measure, prep, style, and troubleshoot whenever needed—including Joel Stovall, Anna Lorein, Francisco Carcamo, Yolanda Mejia, and Kevin Lee.

Special thanks to:
Andy Villaluna, for killing it since day one and always doing it with a joke and a smile. Sal Vasquez, who has become known around here as the Maestro. Genevieve Hardison, who works crazy hard and always makes sure the restau-rants run as smoothly as possible. And Tom Gilmore and Jerri Perrone for giving a chef his big break.

The whole Chronicle team, including Sarah Billingsley for believing in this book and shepherding the journey and Vanessa Dina for her design vision. To both for always being so patient, kind, and understanding.

Kitty Cowles, who made this book happen, and for her support, energy, and high standards. Couldn't imagine doing this without you.

Dylan James Ho and Jeni Afuso, for all of the care that went into the photos, the shared meals, and steadfast friendship.

Thanks also to Dawn Yanagihara and Jane Tunks Demel for all the detailed checking and double-checking.

And to our dogs Bear and Winston, who kept us company during many late nights of talking and writing and cooking.

DEDICATION FROM JOSEF CENTENO

For my grandparents and parents, who showed me the importance of work ethic and persistence and never giving up.

INTRODUCTION 12

CHAPTER 1
spicy | salty | pickled | preserved 20
Mint and rose pickled red onions 22

Pickled rooibos grapes 24

Curry leaf Meyer lemon pickle 26

Sweet-and-sour huckleberries 28

Pickled huckleberries 29

Quick cherry "almostarda" 30

Pomegranate and Concord grape molasses 32

Fennel honey 33

Baharat 35

Berberé 36

Urfa biber shichimi togarashi 38

Arbol-guajillo furikake 39

Coffee-spice rub 40

Harrough 42

Dukkah many ways 45

Caraway croutons 54

Bacon bread crumb persillade 55

Walnut-miso bagna cauda 56

Sunflower-miso tahini 58

Muhammara 59

Mortar-and-pestle romesco 60

Mortar-and-pestle harissa 62

Salbitxada 63

Adjika vinaigrette 64

Salmorejo 66

Fenugreek-chipotle tomato sauce 67

Chermou-lata 68

Mint and fines herbes salsa verde 70

Lime and fish sauce vinaigrette 71

Juniper-tarragon vinaigrette 72

Creamy juniper-tarragon tahini dressing 73

"Broken" cipollini-buttermilk dressing 74

Dashi concentrate 76

Yuzu-dashi vinaigrette 77

Poblano-feta dip 79

Kochkocha 82

Chimichurri 84

Mexican sriracha 85

Ghee 86

Aonori mascarpone butter 88

Yogurt in a jar 90

Fresh ricotta 91

Cacik 92

Crème fraîche 94

Creamy dill dressing 95

CHAPTER 2
fresh | green | snappy | light 96
Castelfranco with cheddar and miso-fenugreek dressing 98

Cabbage slaw with crème fraîche, mitsuba, and kochkocha 102

Red endive and blood oranges with blue cheese, dukkah, and Banyuls vinaigrette 104

Snap pea and Asian pear salad with grapefruit, burrata, and hazelnuts 107

Tuscan melon and Persian cucumber salad with cacik 110

Salted cucumbers with avocado and ginger-soy dressing 112

Fennel, kale, shaved cauliflower, and apple with creamy dill dressing and bacon bread crumb persillade 113

Crudités with walnut-miso bagna cauda 114

Blistered green beans with fenugreek-chipotle tomato sauce 116

CHAPTER 3

bright | citrusy | zesty | hardy
118

Creamy Romanesco soup with grapefruit, nigella, and fresh horseradish 120

Roasted Romanesco and Treviso radicchio with yuzu and dashi 122

"Caesar" Brussels sprouts 125

Kohlrabi with crème fraîche, mint, lemon, and yuzu kosho 128

Flowering choy with lime and fish sauce vinaigrette 130

Caramelized cauliflower with mint, pine nuts, lime, and yogurt 132

Sautéed broccolini with Mexican sriracha and queso fresco 134

Baked fenugreek-nigella pork and beef meatballs 135

Tuscan kale with crushed fenugreek-nigella meatballs and sherry raisins 137

CHAPTER 4

buttery | crispy | tangy | herbal
142

Griddled corn cake with aonori mascarpone butter 144

Jicama salad with mango, fennel, cucumber, peanuts, and lime and fish sauce vinaigrette 147

Panko-crusted shrimp with chives and Mexican sriracha 148

Potato croquettes 151

Hamachi crudo with adjika, yuzu-dashi vinaigrette, avocado, and potato croquettes 154

Coffee-rubbed beef carpaccio with juniper-tarragon vinaigrette and crispy shallots 157

Panfried rainbow trout with brown butter, Meyer lemon, green olives, and chives 160

Citrus and dry-cured olive salad 163

Slow-roasted berberé-cured ocean trout with lemon tempura and citrus and olive salad 166

Tomato-dill pappardelle with caraway bread crumbs 169

Lengua "schnitzel" with brown butter, capers, and cherry tomatoes 172

Bäco flatbread 175

CHAPTER 5

earthy | sharp | velvety | savory
180

Beets bi tahina 182

English pea and dill "hummus" 184

Fuyu persimmon salad with grapes, red walnuts, and sherry vinegar 186

Sweet potatoes with aonori mascarpone butter, feta, and honey 188

Rutabaga and pancetta with lemon, anchovy, and capers 190

Bulgur pancakes with grape leaves, raisins, and goat cheese 193

Eggplant with avocado, Persian cucumbers, herbs, and cipollini-buttermilk dressing 194

Berberé chicken and creamy Pecorino rice 196

Hand-torn pasta 201

Hand-torn pasta with yuzu, dashi, and brown butter 204

Pork belly with sujuk spices and hand-torn pasta 207

CHAPTER 6

creamy | nutty | crunchy | floral 210

Barley porridge with ginger and sautéed oranges 212

Chilled buttermilk-cacik soup with dill and walnuts 214

Poblano soup with pancetta and pickled grapes 216

Roasted golden beets with radishes, cucumbers, hazelnuts, and creamy poblano-feta dressing 218

Sautéed peaches and shishito peppers with goat cheese, cashews, and saffron honey 221

Orange-scented creamed spigarello with almonds and Aleppo pepper 224

Eggplant purée with sumac and garlic 226

Fava "hummus" with mint and Pecorino cheese 227

Lebni with eggplant purée, fava "hummus," and za'atar 228

Imjadra with cherries, parsley, sumac yogurt, and fried shallots 230

Braised chicken with leeks, tomatoes, berberé, thyme, and yogurt 234

Creamy grits with blistered tomatoes, pickled serrano chiles, and sunflower-miso tahini 238

Nigella-lavender albacore with ume and tomatoes 241

CHAPTER 7

tender | juicy | peppery | rich 244

Sichuan pepper lamb top round with English pea and parsley salad 246

Skirt steak with horseradish yogurt and beets bi tahina 249

Chicken escabeche with mint 252

Smoked paprika beef shoulder braised with shiitake-lemongrass broth 255

Baharat-spiced porchetta 258

Cumin-spiced beef and lamb patties with pine nuts and raisins 260

Lamb and tomato stew with chickpeas and curry leaf Meyer lemon pickle 262

Berberé double-cut lamb chops 264

Whole roasted orange- and soy-glazed duck 267

Coffee-rubbed prime rib with mint and rose pickled red onions 270

CHAPTER 8

flaky | fruity | caramely | tart 272

Strawberry-elderflower fool **274**

Buttermilk wheat biscuit with strawberry-elderflower fool **276**

Salty caramel **279**

Canela rice pudding with salty caramel and orange blossom cream **280**

Pistachio cheesecake custards with matcha sugar and kataifi **283**

Yogurt panna cotta with pickled huckleberries **288**

Blueberry and frangipane rye-caraway crostata **290**

Blackberry sesame cake with cardamom sugar **293**

CHAPTER 9

bubbly | sweet | sour | vivid 294

Sudachi-cucumber yogurt drink **298**

Watermelon-lime–white pepper yogurt drink **298**

Rosewater-pistachio yogurt drink **299**

Tangerine-mint yogurt drink **299**

Ginger syrup **302**

Cherry-mint fruit mash **302**

Blackberry–Thai basil fruit mash **303**

Strawberry-tarragon fruit mash **303**

Celery shrub **306**

Grapefruit-dill shrub **307**

Peach-sumac shrub **307**

INDEX 308

Introduction

DOWNTOWN LOS ANGELES

Downtown is the vibrant, pulsing, always evolving heart of Los Angeles. Its boundaries are roughly the L.A. River and a couple of crisscrossing freeways, and in between are about five square miles that make up downtown. Parts are gritty, parts are shiny and new, and all of it's majestic.

At the intersection of Fourth and Main Streets in an area known as the Historic Core, I opened five restaurants in five years: Bäco Mercat, Bar Amá, Orsa & Winston, Ledlow, and P.Y.T., in that order.

A lot has changed since the start. When I opened Bäco Mercat in a 110-year-old Italian Renaissance Revival building called the San Fernando in 2011, it was on a dicey corner on the border between Gallery Row and Skid Row. Now the block is full of boutiques, renovated lofts, nightclubs, and sushi bars.

But the streets around here still look a lot like they did more than a hundred years ago. The Historic Core is known for its early twentieth-century buildings: the city's first skyscraper, its original stock exchange, and dozens more landmarks. Every Saturday morning, by coincidence, a walking tour of historic downtown starts directly in front of Bäco Mercat as servers are setting up the patio for brunch.

Up until the second half of the last century, the neighborhood was the entertainment and financial center of the city, filled with big banks, grand hotels, and movie palaces like the Orpheum and Million Dollar Theater. Think dripping chandeliers, opulent ballrooms, and Beaux Arts or Art Deco facades along tree-lined streets.

But after World War II, the movie houses shifted to Hollywood Boulevard, and the banks relocated to high-rises uphill and farther west. Residents left for the suburbs, and businesses shuttered. Downtown was abandoned, hit by an epidemic of drugs and prostitution.

Now in the middle of a revival, the Historic Core is becoming the greatest neighborhood in L.A. all over again. The corner of Fourth and Main has its own particular charms: a Berlinesque nightclub in an alley behind Bäco Mercat, a Shepard Fairey mural around the corner, and the Regent Theater—one of L.A.'s first movie palaces and now an always-packed concert venue—down the street.

On any given night, you might bump into a local character like André ("not homeless," he says, "just residentially challenged"), who will either invite you to karaoke or ask you for change, or Gwyneth Paltrow, hopping onto the curb from the back seat of a black Mercedes G-Class.

If you look skyward, you'll see strung white lights zigzagging across the tops of buildings. Across the street from Bäco Mercat and Ledlow is the former Farmers and Merchants Bank (the future site of a contemporary art museum), built to resemble a Roman temple. Kitty-corner is the old Barclay Hotel, which has seen better days but is still a popular film location, especially as a Manhattan stand-in (its lobby was the café in *As Good as It Gets,* a coffee shop in *500 Days of Summer,* and a casino in *Inception*).

Before opening Bäco Mercat, I cooked Spanish-influenced small plates in West Hollywood, $10-a-course tasting menus at a restaurant in Koreatown, from the tiny kitchen of an Echo Park café with just my sous chef and me as pretty much the entire staff, and at a Little Tokyo canteen and bar, where every night we knocked out several dozen specials scrawled out on two big chalkboards for hundreds of covers.

And then I landed here in the middle of downtown. It's where I live and work, with five restaurants and a loft in a one-block radius. I walk to work every morning. I go home in the middle of the afternoon between lunch and dinner service to take my dogs to the park. And every night I am at each of the restaurants, cooking on the line at one or more, and checking in at the others.

There's no other part of Los Angeles like this one. Lightning-fast change plays out against a backdrop of turn-of-the-century architecture. And no neighborhood is as mixed—old, young, up-and-coming, down-and-out, of all cultures and persuasions. Everyone fits in.

It's also a fitting neighborhood for an unlikely group of restaurants, each with its own spin on idiosyncratic flavors.

THE RESTAURANTS

The first time I saw the space that would be Bäco Mercat, I knew it was right. I loved the bones of the place, with its remnants of marble walls and high brass-framed windows. I washed those windows myself, painted the walls, and polished the brass and marble. I was focused on making it happen—even if I had to do it with only a hot plate and whiskey served in paper cups. Luckily, it has a real kitchen and bar, an always-growing menu, and customers that spill out onto the sidewalk.

I had opened during an economic downturn, and figured I'd keep the menu casual, focusing on the namesake flatbread sandwich called a Bäco and its several iterations. I had a small staff, and we'd roll the naan-like flatbreads out by hand each day, filling them with pork belly, crispy beef "carnitas" (traditionally made with pork), fava bean fritters, or chicken escabeche, along with any combination of the dozen sauces always on the line. But within a week, the menu doubled, then it tripled, and quadrupled.

It's still constantly evolving. The kitchen is kind of a workshop of freewheeling bold flavors from Spain, North and East Africa, the Eastern Mediterranean, Eastern Europe, and parts of Asia, with the emphasis on freewheeling. The goal isn't authenticity but deliciousness.

Less than a year after Bäco Mercat opened, I built Bar Amá around the corner, a homage to the Tex-Mex cooking I grew up with—my versions of the food that my mom, grandmothers, and great-grandmother cooked. (The restaurant is named after my great-grandmother, who lived to be nearly ninety years old; we called her Amá, which basically means "the boss lady.") We serve green enchiladas, chiles rellenos, and migas—the tortilla chips with scrambled eggs that we'd eat for breakfast every Saturday. The margaritas flow, and sure, there are the traditional breakfast tacos, queso, and fajitas of San Antonio.

But I couldn't help but start spinning out more flavors: jicama salad with lots of lime and fish sauce; cauliflower tossed in cilantro pesto with cashews, lime, and Cotija cheese; slow-roasted beef belly with tomatillo and pomegranate seeds.

The following year, Orsa & Winston opened next to Bar Amá. I'd been itching to return to my fine-dining roots, so I installed a wood-burning oven in a thirty-seat restaurant and offered a menu inspired by Japanese and Italian ingredients. The kitchen melds flavors and techniques both experimental and ancient: inoculating koji, making miso and naturally leavened breads, grilling over bincho-tan. The menu is also inspired by travels in Japan and Italy: Kyoto's Nishiki Market, Salumeria Giusti in Modena and Salumeria Roscioli in Rome, the cardoon fields in Piedmont, or the sushi-ya in Ginza.

Not long after, I was offered a big, bright location on the southeast corner of Fourth and

Main, also known as Woody Guthrie Square. (Woody Guthrie moved to downtown L.A. in the 1930s and worked as a dishwasher and sang on street corners, including this one.) And so Ledlow and P.Y.T. followed. The first is a café and bar with twists on American classics, and with the same attention to seasonality, unexpected ingredients, and flavor as the first three restaurants. P.Y.T. is a vegetable-focused restaurant, inspired by a local school's farm in nearby Lincoln Heights. A few cooks from the restaurants and I volunteered to help terrace the hillside and plant seeds on half an acre, where the farm manager grows heirloom tomatoes, Japanese red mustard, several varieties of turnips, radishes of all kinds, runner beans, and arugula and mitsuba and all their buds. All the flavors of the seasons.

Flavor first is of course the philosophy behind all of my restaurants. And the spirit of each restaurant is rooted in the way unexpected flavors and ingredients are combined.

I write all of the menus—lunch, brunch, dinner, twenty-course tastings. There are several signature dishes included in this book, mainly from Bäco Mercat. But this isn't a cookbook with recipes from any single restaurant. Many are inspired by dishes at the restaurants or are entirely new, especially because the menus always change depending on the availability or discovery of ingredients. In spirit, *Bäco* is about all of them, a snapshot of the daily whirl of flavors on this downtown corner.

ABOUT THE FLAVORS

I have always daydreamed about flavors, by way of ingredients, seasons, and cultures. Before I ever traveled to Spain, I could taste the Iberian sauces romesco, salbitxada, and salmorejo the way I fantasized about them. I imagined and reimagined Yemeni zhoug, Abkhazian adjika, and North African chermoula. And these became an integral part of the way I cooked.

I like the Ethiopian spice mixture berberé right along with the salt and pepper on my table, so that I can add it to fresh pasta with tomato sauce or a juicy thick-cut pork chop. When I make pozole, the broth has the flavors of the Southwest and of North Africa. One of my favorite marinades is garlic mashed in a mortar with coriander, nigella, dried fenugreek leaves, Aleppo pepper, and Japanese miso.

Is it fusion? I don't know. I think it's Los Angeles food, a crazy quilt knitted together from immigrant experience, imagination, and the pursuit of flavor. I come from an immigrant family, grew up with the melting-pot cuisine that is Tex-Mex, worked my way through French kitchens in New York, cooked with chefs inspired by Japanese kaiseki and Spanish modernism, and moved to California to chase my dreams (and some of the best vegetables in America!).

I grew up in San Antonio, where the culinary blending of cultures was Tex-Mex. For me, that meant the pequin chiles my grandmother grew, pickled onions on everything, *borracho* beans with smoked ham hock, green enchiladas, *carne guisada* (braised beef with tomatoes and lots of cumin, garlic, and chili powder), and the turkey from the mesquite-burning brick smoker in Ms. Miller's backyard. My role model was my great-grandmother, who fled Guanajuato during the Mexican Revolution and could make a delicious meal from just fideo and a tomato.

I come from a very big family of mixed heritage—Mexican, Spanish, Irish, French, English, German, and Polish—a family of grocers, butchers, and barbecuers. We'd number more than one hundred at some family gatherings, and there would be beef ribs, pork ribs, steaks, and cabrito (whole goat). Robust flavors I knew. And loved. Cumin, cilantro, chiles—the stuff of Tejano cuisine.

I wasn't exposed to the gastronomic experiences of traveling abroad. But once I discovered cookbooks, I was transported to the Middle East, the Mediterranean, Africa, and beyond. As a culinary student in New York, I pored over them, mostly as references to the ingredients of other cuisines.

Culinaria Spain was big, yellow-covered, and filled with glossy pictures and recipes for the regional dishes that would later inspire my own versions. Paula Wolfert's *Cooking of the Eastern Mediterranean* was like a bible with its pomegranate sauces, Georgian pies, and Macedonian salads. In André Soltner's *Lutèce Cookbook* were culinary life lessons: "When I start to cook something, I already have in my mouth, and in my mind, the taste of what I am cooking. It is like a dream, a dream of what the food is going to be." I started thinking about food and cooking that way.

As much as I aspired to cook like a chef in a Michelin three-star restaurant, I also wanted to cook like an Andalusian rancher, a fishmonger in Niigata, and a grandmother from Tbilisi—maybe all rolled into one!—even though at the time I'd never been to southern Spain, western Japan, or central Georgia.

I imagined what those dishes might be like, and I created them to taste exactly the way I thought they should—maybe that isn't entirely accurate. Then and now, I make food to taste exactly the way I *want*, with the goal that any and all flavors should taste as if they were always meant to be together.

I didn't set out to be weird or intend to be offhand. I respect ingredients and traditions. There are reasons that certain flavors go together: katsuobushi and konbu, cilantro and lime, garlic and oregano. But I don't stick to convention.

This is all to say: follow inspiration. You don't have to travel to Chengdu to appreciate *ma la* (the tingling sensation brought on by Sichuan peppercorns) or to Addis Ababa to love the Ethiopian hot sauce kochkocha. I don't think you have to go to culinary school to learn how to combine flavors. And for the most part, you don't need much more than a good knife and a mortar and pestle (and a thermometer). I cook from instinct. And I've learned to do this by tasting again and again and again.

Imagination is the first step toward fully realized flavor, when seasoning brings ingredients to life. I try to navigate what's at hand—chiles, seeds, nuts, vinegars, oils, spices, herbs, vegetables, meat—in order to reach new heights of sweet, sour, earthy, bitter, nutty, piquant, marine, grassy, floral, and so on. Sparked by these, I begin to taste in my head. Rather than strictly following the customs of any one cuisine in particular, I draw from a lot of cultures, especially with sauces and spices. Chimichurri and harissa. Yuzu kosho and cacik. I think these condiments can be the building blocks of flavor.

I like them in unique combinations, and I think they work when technique is a foundation. It's important to appreciate the classics. These were hammered into me while working my way through the kitchen brigade system at New York restaurants such as Daniel, Vong, Les Célébrités, and La Côte Basque.

But after moving to California's Bay Area, I stepped away from the velouté and demiglace while working at Charles Nob Hill and then at Manresa. My aim was to cook simply and to get out of the way of the best possible ingredients. I was responsible for ordering the product for tasting menus with up to thirty courses, and I had carte blanche. This freedom opened the floodgates to new ideas, ingredients, and flavors.

There is one question that all of the cooks in the kitchens regularly ask themselves at Bäco Mercat, Bar Amá, Orsa & Winston, Ledlow, and P.Y.T.: "Is it *chingòn*?" The direct translation from Spanish slang isn't exactly family-friendly. It means, "Is it fucking great?" But to everyone here, it means so much more. It's automatically assumed that everything is properly seasoned and is balanced with acid. But beyond that, does it set off fireworks? Does it have the most flavor those ingredients can give? Does it have character? Does your palate feel a "pow"?

ABOUT THE RECIPES

I think the "pow!" in my cooking comes from layers of flavor, from citrus, herbs, vinegar, and spices. I like contrasts of fat, acid, textures, temperatures, traditions, and techniques. This is how a dish comes together—the crunch and creaminess of it, the savoriness, the nod to inspiring cuisines—because flavors go beyond our sense of taste, beyond salty, sweet, bitter, sour, and umami. They require and stimulate all of our senses.

Contrast and balance are also what make flavors work well together. So this book is organized into groups of contrasting flavors and textures, and the chapters progress from lighter to heavier: raw and crunchy greens (leafy and not), sturdier and earthier vegetables and grains, meat, and desserts. That's a rough outline; there's a lot in between.

Many of the dishes in this book cannot be categorized readily, inspired as much by Middle Eastern mezze as Italian contorni, snacks at a Japanese izakaya, or Mom's Sunday supper. But they easily can be combined to make a meal—a salad of something "fresh, green, snappy, light" with a roast that's "tender, juicy, peppery, rich," for example. The categories are considered but flexible. The aim is balance, so that a lot of flavors can go together. Baharat-spiced porchetta (page 258) with a salad of eggplant, avocado, Persian cucumbers, and a "broken" cipollini-

buttermilk dressing (page 74). Handmade pasta with brown butter and yuzu (page 204) to go with skirt steak and a hummus-like dip of beets bi tahina (page 182). Or imjadra (lentils and bulgur) with cherries, sumac yogurt, and fried shallots (page 230) as a side dish for braised chicken with leeks, tomatoes, Ethiopian spices, and thyme (page 234).

I use a lot of spices. I guess I've never considered not toasting and grinding my own spices whenever possible. My favorite piece of cooking equipment at home is a big marble mortar and pestle. It holds almost 3 liquid cups and weighs about 15 pounds—more than one of my dogs! Grinding spices with it is easy, and it connects me to a custom that dates to antiquity. It's amazing that a tool that seems to slow down time is also extremely efficient and nearly as fast as an electric spice grinder (and easier to clean).

I also use a lot of fresh herbs: parsley, dill, tarragon, chervil, chives, mint. I always have the combination of finely chopped shallots, chives, and grated lemon zest around for adding a hit of flavor to a dish during the last minute of cooking, or as a garnish. (At the restaurants, we call it trio mix.) Sometimes I call for a lot of herbs in one dish. If you don't have one in particular on hand, skip it; in a lot of cases, you could rely on parsley or mint or celery leaves instead.

The recipes here aren't unadulterated versions of authentic dishes. They are personal "inspired by" dishes, or made-up-altogether dishes. So I'm definitely not going to tell you that the way I put together certain flavors is the one and only way. I try to offer suggestions for substitutions, alternatives, and variations. Even if I don't, I would advocate not immediately giving up on a recipe if you're missing a specific ingredient, such as curry leaves or fenugreek or

Japanese sesame paste. Instead, you could substitute a bay leaf or oregano or tahini, respectively.

Sometimes it's a good thing. You stumble upon a different flavor that you might like better. (One caveat: Whatever you add, add a little at a time. If you add too much, you can't take it away.) We should all have the courage to try something we've never made before.

You also could use part of a recipe that speaks to you. Some long recipes I've broken into parts: fenugreek meatballs (page 135), for example, for a dish of Tuscan kale with crushed meatballs and roasted radishes (page 137). Or eggplant purée with sumac and garlic (page 226) for an appetizer of lebni, eggplant purée, and fava hummus (page 228). And many of the condiments in the first chapter are easy to incorporate into your repertoire: mint and rose pickled onions (page 22), cherry "almostarda" (page 30), aonori mascarpone butter (page 88). Or maybe a flavor combination will inspire you—tomato and Japanese pickled plum with nigella and lavender (page 241), oranges and olives (page 163), yuzu and dashi (page 204), miso and walnuts (page 114), cumin and cardamom (page 260), Sichuan pepper and coriander (page 246).

The recipes are themes on flavors, sometimes unorthodox combinations from a lot of cuisines: Spanish, Italian, Japanese, Mexican, French, Middle Eastern, South American, African. "Cultural oscillations," one writer once called them. "Not so much fusion as utter reinvention."

They're meant to inspire creativity and aren't meant to be rigid formulas. They require focusing on the details of technique, but they're flexible enough to accommodate adjusting for taste. Because ultimately we're all on the same voyage of discovery.

A FEW NOTES

Throughout the book, butter is unsalted, flour is organic all-purpose (measured by spooning the flour into the cup), and salt is kosher, unless listed otherwise.

I've thought a lot about which oils are best for cooking. These are oils with a high smoke point, mild flavor, and a relatively low percentage of polyunsaturated fats—the less refined the oil, the better. In general, for sautéing and frying, I use avocado oil. Like olive oil, it's one of the few oils extracted directly from the fruit, rather than chemically extracted from the seed. Another great option is rice bran oil. But avocado and rice bran oil are expensive compared with olive oil, which is a good substitute. Occasionally, I prefer olive oil for its flavor over the more neutral avocado oil. I use extra-virgin olive oil for salads and dressings.

One spice blend I don't make myself is za'atar. Za'atar is the name of an herb that grows wild throughout the Eastern Mediterranean. It's also the name for the blend that includes za'atar, ground sumac, and sesame seeds. The herb's flavor is similar to summer savory's, but it isn't exactly the same. So I prefer to use blends that hew closer to the original; you can buy it at a local spice shop or online from Penzeys, Kalustyan's, Formaggio Kitchen, Le Sanctuaire, World Spice Merchants, and La Boîte. These are good online sources for other blends and chiles, such as the Turkish pepper urfa biber.

Several recipes in this book call for Aleppo pepper. It's the oily, fruity, bright red pepper from the Aleppo region in Syria. But because of the crisis in Syria, what's imported to the United States is probably from Turkey's Maras area. It is still for the most part labeled Aleppo pepper, which is what's listed here.

Sauces, marinades, pickles, preserves, dressings, and condiments are the best way to deliver concentrated seasoning, and the possible combinations of salt, acid, herbs, zests, chiles, and spices are endless. They provide gigantic potential for a lot of robust flavors and are the most direct path to creativity. Sauces and condiments crisscross spicy with floral, salty with bitter, tart with sweet. An inventory of them facilitates combining flavors, cuisines, traditions, textures, and colors.

I've always loved sauces because they are specific to regions, families, and individuals. They're the way I connect to the personal view of a cook—and to my own personal view. My grandmother's salsa was never like anyone else's. Grandma Alice grew pequin chiles in her front yard and would crush them using a mortar and pestle, adding just lime juice, garlic, and salt, skipping tomatoes altogether. The signature to my great-grandmother Amá's cooking was her simple sofrito of diced carrots, onions, and potatoes, instead of the traditional peppers and tomatoes in a lot of Tejano cooking.

For me, these were windows into cooks' souls. At the same time, I also saw sauces and spice mixtures as windows into other cultures. Spain figured profoundly in my cooking from the time I learned about salbitxada and romesco, two almond, tomato, and pepper sauces of the port city Tarragona. And that was before I'd even been to Catalonia, where the way each cook prepares romesco is a badge of identity—with tomatoes or not; Ñora peppers or sweet paprika; sherry vinegar or lemon juice; almonds, hazelnuts, or bread crumbs.

The first time I went to Kyoto, I visited more spice shops than temples, tracking down dozens of variations of shichimi togarashi, the Japanese spice mixture that typically includes dried red chiles, roasted sesame seeds, dried yuzu zest, hempseeds, poppy seeds, dried seaweed, and sansho pepper. There are a few shops that will custom-blend shichimi according to your taste (whether you like more sansho or seaweed or chiles, for example) from dozens of ingredients, including dried sour plum, dried tangerine, ginger, shiso, and cherry blossoms.

One of the things that was always important to me: discovering my own style as a chef. Part of that comes with making flavors one's own. It's probably every cook's impulse. For example, there are seemingly infinite ways to tweak the amounts of each spice and herb in the Georgian recipe for khmeli suneli, traditionally a combination of dill, mint, parsley, coriander, marjoram, fenugreek, marigold, hyssop, thyme, basil, saffron, pepper, and/or bay leaves. By tasting and adjusting, you settle on the version that's yours.

I respect tradition and imagination equally, but above all, I believe taste is tantamount. And my main motivation, in cooking and eating, is pleasure. If your heart desires more cumin in the baharat (a Middle Eastern spice blend), no rosebuds in the pickles, Virginia peanuts instead of pistachios in the Egyptian nut-and-seed mixture dukkah, it's okay to listen to it.

spicy

salty

pickled

preserved

Mint and rose pickled red onions

I've always used pickled onions almost as a seasoning, for their sharpness and pungency, as well as to add texture. This probably goes back to when I was a kid in San Antonio. Pickled onions were the ubiquitous condiment with barbecue we picked up from Ms. Miller's, a backyard operation where Ms. Miller and her sister smoked ribs, brisket, and whole turkeys. Hers were fat rings of pickled white onions spiked with oregano. But these slivers of pickled red onion draw inspiration from both Middle Eastern and Mexican flavors: mint and rosebud and serrano chile. They're simultaneously piquant and spicy and slightly sweet. Use them in salads or sandwiches, with grilled meat, on top of cubed feta along with olive oil and a pile of herbs for a quick appetizer, or in your Bloody Marys.

NOTE: Dried rosebuds are available in some Middle Eastern markets and spice shops as well as online. If you don't happen to have any rosebuds, these pickled onions are delicious without them.

MAKES ABOUT 1¼ CUPS [205 G]

1 medium red onion
½ serrano chile, seeded
½ habanero chile, seeded (optional)
¾ cup [180 ml] red wine vinegar
¼ cup [60 ml] olive oil
1½ tsp sugar
½ tsp salt
6 fresh mint leaves
6 fresh basil leaves
1 dried rosebud
Fresh black pepper

Cut the red onion, serrano chile, and habanero chile (if using) into thin slices. Place the onion in a heatproof bowl and set aside.

Heat the vinegar, oil, chiles, sugar, and salt in a small saucepan over high heat until boiling. Once it reaches a boil, remove from the heat. Pour the vinegar mixture over the onion.

Tear the mint and basil and stir into the onion and vinegar mixture. Crumble the rosebud into the mixture. Add 3 grinds of black pepper. Use immediately or store in a covered container in the refrigerator for up to 1 week.

Pickled rooibos grapes

Crunchy-tart pickled grapes are more than a garnish. They bring sweet and tart and juicy and crunchy to a dish all at the same time. Use any type of seedless grape, cut in half so that they absorb the pickling liquid. The rooibos tea adds complexity to the spiced pickling brine. I use these grapes a lot, to complement smoked meats, pasta salads, creamy soups, and green salads.

MAKES ABOUT 2 CUPS [540 G]

1 cinnamon stick
1 star anise
½ tsp black peppercorns
½ tsp coriander seeds
½ tsp fennel seeds
½ cup [100 g] sugar
½ cup [120 ml] water
½ cup [120 ml] apple cider vinegar
1 Tbsp rooibos tea leaves
9 oz [250 g] red seedless grapes, halved lengthwise

Prepare an ice bath by filling a large bowl with ice water. Place a heat-proof container or jar large enough to hold the grapes into the ice. Set aside.

Put the cinnamon stick, star anise, black peppercorns, coriander, and fennel seeds in a saucepan and heat over medium heat just until they begin to release some of their oils, 30 to 60 seconds. Add the sugar, water, and vinegar. Stir the mixture and bring it to a boil.

Remove from the heat. Stir in the rooibos tea and steep for 2 minutes. Carefully strain the hot pickling liquid into the container or jar in the ice bath, discarding the cinnamon stick, star anise, and the peppercorns and seeds. Let the pickling liquid cool until lukewarm; it shouldn't be hot or it will blister the grape skins.

Add the grapes to the lukewarm pickling liquid. Use immediately or store in a covered container in the refrigerator for up to 3 days.

Curry leaf Meyer lemon pickle

A riff on preserved lemons, this quick version is spiced with curry leaves, habanero chile, and black and yellow mustard seeds. This lemon pickle can be used in any recipe where you would use traditional preserved lemon (which normally takes a few weeks to ferment), the staple ingredient in so many Moroccan dishes. I use these in salads, soups, and tagines, and as a garnish or condiment for roasts and grilled steaks or fish. Use fresh curry leaves rather than dried to get the most out of the herb's flavor. Once cooked, they soften and can be eaten but are usually discarded. As the lemons cook, they take on the curry leaves' citrus-anise-peppery flavor (also reminiscent of asafetida); habanero's floral heat; and the pungency of mustard seeds.

NOTE: Curry leaves are available at some Indian markets, farmers' markets, and online.

MAKES ABOUT 1 CUP [235 G]

2 Meyer lemons

2 Tbsp avocado or olive oil

2 tsp yellow mustard seeds

2 tsp black mustard seeds

8 fresh curry leaves

¼ cup [60 ml] apple cider vinegar

½ habanero chile, seeded and cut into very thin slices

1 tsp chopped dill fronds

Cut the Meyer lemons into very thin slices with a sharp knife or mandoline and set aside.

Heat the oil in a saucepan over medium heat until hot and shimmering; its high sides will help prevent oil from splattering when the mustard seeds are added. Carefully add the yellow and black mustard seeds—they'll start to pop right away—and then the curry leaves. Immediately, but slowly, pour in the vinegar, then add the habanero and the lemon slices.

Turn the heat to high and bring the mixture to a boil, then immediately remove from the heat. Pour into a heatproof jar or container and cool slightly. Gently stir in the dill. Use immediately or cover the jar or container and store in the refrigerator for up to 1 week.

Sweet-and-sour huckleberries

Everybody loves huckleberry season, which comes when summer turns into fall. The tiny, tart blue-black berries are native to the Pacific Coast, among a couple of other places, and I'd never had them until I moved to California. Huckleberries are great in either sweet or savory dishes, versatile, and sturdy. Unlike a lot of other berries, such as strawberries, blueberries, and raspberries, they retain their integrity and shape when cooked (i.e., they don't break down much or explode). Adding sugar and vinegar to make a gastrique (sweet-and-sour sauce) or a pickle (recipe follows) amplifies their flavor—and preserves them for a little longer. Serve either the gastrique or pickle with meat and poultry dishes—roast duck, venison, lamb, quail, squab, beef, or pork, such as baharat-spiced porchetta (page 258).

MAKES ABOUT 1 CUP [205 G]

1 cinnamon stick
1 cup [200 g] sugar
½ cup [120 ml] sherry vinegar
¾ cup [125 g] fresh or frozen huckleberries
½ tsp salt
½ tsp freshly ground black pepper
1 sprig summer savory (optional)
One 1-in- [2.5-cm-] wide strip Meyer lemon peel (optional)

Toast the cinnamon stick in a small, dry frying pan over medium heat, tossing occasionally, until fragrant, about 2 minutes. Remove from the heat and set aside.

Heat the sugar in a saucepan over medium heat, moving it around with a wooden spoon or heatproof spatula so that it cooks evenly without too much stirring. Cook until it is completely melted and caramel colored, 3 to 5 minutes.

Turn off the heat. Standing back from the pan, carefully add the vinegar a spoonful at a time; it will cause the mixture to seize, froth, and steam. Once the steam subsides, return the heat to medium and add the huckleberries, cinnamon stick, salt, and black pepper, stirring to combine. Simmer the mixture for 2 minutes so that the flavors meld. Remove from the heat, drop in the savory and lemon peel, if using, and cool. Discard the cinnamon stick, savory, and lemon peel. Use immediately or store in a covered container in the refrigerator for up to 3 weeks.

Pickled huckleberries

MAKES ABOUT ⅔ CUP [140 G]

1 cinnamon stick

½ Tbsp black peppercorns

⅓ cup [65 g] sugar

⅓ cup [80 ml] water

⅓ cup [80 ml] rice vinegar

½ cup [85 g] fresh or frozen huckleberries

½ tsp salt

1 or 2 rose geranium leaves or 5 leaves lemon verbena (optional)

Toast the cinnamon stick and peppercorns in a small, dry frying pan over medium heat, stirring occasionally, until fragrant, about 2 minutes. Tie them up in cheesecloth to make a sachet.

Put the sachet, sugar, water, and vinegar in a saucepan and bring to a boil over medium-high heat. Lower the heat and simmer for 2 to 3 minutes.

Add the huckleberries, turn the heat to medium-high, and bring the mixture back to a boil. Lower the heat again and simmer until thickened, 3 to 4 minutes. Add the salt. Remove from the heat, drop in the rose geranium or lemon verbena leaves, if using, and cool. Discard the sachet and leaves. Use immediately or store in a covered container in the refrigerator for up to 3 weeks.

Quick cherry "almostarda"

Mostarda is the mystical candied fruit condiment of northern Italy. I say mystical because its traditional preparation is ritualistic and exacting, preserving the fruit whole by steeping it in a sugar syrup that's reduced once a day over a few days until nearly transparent. Then the preserved fruit is flavored with mustard—its seeds or powder or volatile oil. This recipe is a quick version, an agrodolce (sweet-sour) version prepared like a gastrique with caramelized sugar and vinegar. The cherries taste fresh, and the syrup is complex, with added mustard seeds and spicy horseradish. I use it as a condiment for roasts or with cheeses.

MAKES 1 CUP [270 G]

¾ cup [140 g] stemmed pitted cherries

½ cup [100 g] sugar

½ cup [120 ml] white wine or Champagne vinegar

1 tsp yellow mustard seeds

1 tsp strained prepared horseradish

1 tsp chopped fresh tarragon

Pinch of salt

½ tsp fresh lemon juice

Put the cherries in a medium heatproof bowl and set aside.

Heat the sugar in a saucepan over medium-high heat, moving it around with a wooden spoon or heatproof spatula so that it cooks evenly without too much stirring. Cook until it is completely melted and dark caramel colored, 5 to 8 minutes.

Turn off the heat. Standing back from the pan, carefully add the vinegar a spoonful at a time; it will cause the mixture to sputter and froth. Return the heat to medium and continue to stir gently until any seized sugar crystals dissolve.

Remove from the heat. Stir in the mustard seeds, horseradish, tarragon, salt, and lemon juice. Pour the mixture over the cherries. Use immediately or store in a covered container in the refrigerator for up to 5 days.

Pomegranate and Concord grape molasses

There's a window between very late summer and very early fall when both pomegranates and Concord grapes are always in the restaurant kitchens. One year, when the Concords were just about overripe and I couldn't seem to go through all the pomegranates I had, I made pomegranate and Concord grape molasses. Pomegranate molasses is pomegranate juice that has been reduced down to a syrup. The traditional Middle Eastern syrup is thick and rich, tangy and not too sweet, and its concentrated flavor makes it musky and complex. Concord grapes aren't as sweet as some other varieties, and their unique foxy, jammy flavor comes through distinctively here. Cook with this molasses as you would pomegranate molasses, such as in stews and braises; use it like honey, drizzled over yogurt, oatmeal, or buttered toast; or mix it into marinades, vinaigrettes, and cocktails.

MAKES 1 CUP [240 G]

8 cups [1.2 kg] pomegranate seeds (from about 6 pomegranates)
4 cups [615 g] Concord grapes

Juice the pomegranate seeds with an electric juicer or juice extractor and strain the juice into a saucepan. You should have about 4 cups [950 ml] pomegranate juice. Then juice the grapes and strain into the same saucepan. You should get about 2 cups [480 ml] grape juice.

Bring the pomegranate and grape juices to a boil over medium-high heat. Turn the heat to medium and simmer until the juice has reduced to a thick syrup, 45 to 60 minutes. It should be about the consistency of maple syrup. Taste as you reduce the syrup; you want a concentrated sweet-tart flavor. If you reduce it too much (it shouldn't be less than 1 cup [240 ml]), it will be bitter. Store in a lidded jar or covered container in the refrigerator for up to 1 month.

VARIATION
Pomegranate and beet molasses: Substitute about 4 cups [950 ml] beet juice (from 4 lb/1.8 kg beets) for the Concord grape juice. Follow the preceding instructions until the juice has reduced to the consistency of maple syrup, about 1½ cups [360 ml].

Fennel honey

Infusing a savory element into honey makes it that much more versatile. In dishes where honey might otherwise be just a little too cloying, it is instead a little more nuanced. Use fennel seeds, fresh thyme or rosemary, saffron threads, long pepper, cubeb pepper, Sichuan pepper, lemon zest, mint, ginger, or dried chiles—these all add another layer of flavor to floral honeys. I use saffron, fennel, or cubeb pepper honey mixed into yogurt or drizzled on fried dishes such as ricotta fritters or crispy battered boquerones (marinated anchovy fillets).

MAKES ½ CUP [150 G]

½ cup [150 g] honey

2 tsp water

½ tsp fennel seeds

Put the honey, water, and fennel seeds in a small saucepan and bring to a simmer over medium-high heat. Simmer for 30 seconds, then immediately remove from the heat. Strain into a small lidded jar and discard the seeds. Store at room temperature for several weeks.

VARIATION

Cubeb honey, saffron honey, and fennel pollen honey: Substitute ½ tsp cubeb pepper, ½ tsp saffron threads mixed with 2 tsp water, or a pinch of fennel pollen for the fennel seeds; stir in the pollen during the last few seconds of heating (do not strain).

Baharat

Baharat is the Arabic word for "spices." Used in the Middle East and North Africa, it's a mixture that often includes cumin, black pepper, paprika, coriander, cloves, nutmeg, cinnamon, and cardamom. Turkish baharat includes dried mint, and my version omits cinnamon. The predominant flavors here are aromatic cumin and coriander, which are especially good with other strong flavors. I like baharat with earthy vegetables, especially eggplant and cauliflower, tomato sauce, and any grilled or roasted meat: rack of lamb, leg of lamb—actually just about any lamb—beefy steaks, stewed short ribs, and roast chicken.

MAKES ABOUT ⅓ CUP [45 G]

2 Tbsp cumin seeds

1 Tbsp coriander seeds

½ tsp cardamom seeds

2 Tbsp freshly ground black pepper

2 Tbsp sweet paprika

1 Tbsp ground cloves

1 Tbsp freshly grated nutmeg

1 Tbsp dried mint (optional)

Toast the cumin, coriander, and cardamom seeds in a small, dry frying pan over medium heat, stirring occasionally, until fragrant, about 2 minutes. Remove from the heat.

Grind the seeds to a coarse powder in a spice grinder or with a mortar and pestle. Transfer to a bowl and combine with the black pepper, paprika, cloves, nutmeg, and dried mint (if using). Store in a covered container in a cool, dark place for up to 1 month.

Berberé

This is not a traditional version of the East African spice blend berberé. My inspiration has always been the mix of dried chiles with my favorite spices. And there are a lot of spices here, but the resulting depth of flavor is worth the small effort of toasting and grinding them. I use berberé (pictured on facing page, center) a lot—in chicken liver mousse, tomato sauce, and homemade sausages, and as a rub for chicken, pork, and lamb. It's great with beans and lentils. Sprinkle it on scrambled eggs or on toast smeared with butter or fresh farmer cheese.

NOTE: You can substitute Aleppo pepper with any coarsely ground, mildly spicy dried chile, such as New Mexico chiles, urfa biber, or cascabel.

MAKES ABOUT ⅔ CUP [80 G]

1½ Tbsp cumin seeds
2 tsp caraway seeds
2 tsp cardamom seeds
2 tsp coriander seeds
1½ Tbsp cubeb pepper
1 tsp whole allspice
½ tsp whole cloves
2 Tbsp dried fenugreek leaves
3 Tbsp Aleppo pepper
2 Tbsp sweet paprika
2 tsp ground ginger
2 tsp ground turmeric
2 tsp salt
1 tsp ground cinnamon

Toast the cumin, caraway, cardamom, and coriander seeds in a small, dry frying pan over medium heat, stirring occasionally, until fragrant, 2 to 3 minutes. Remove from the heat and transfer to a bowl.

Toast the cubeb pepper, allspice, and cloves in the same frying pan over medium heat, stirring occasionally, until fragrant, 2 to 3 minutes. Remove from the heat.

Grind the toasted spices to a coarse powder in a spice grinder or with a mortar and pestle. Return the ground spices to the bowl. Add the fenugreek leaves, Aleppo pepper, paprika, ginger, turmeric, salt, and cinnamon to the bowl of spices. Mix together. Store in a covered container in a cool, dry place for up to 1 month, or freeze in an airtight container for several months.

Urfa biber shichimi togarashi

The translation for the Japanese spice mixture called shichimi togarashi (pictured on page 35, bottom) is "seven-flavor chile pepper," a traditional condiment (originally created by herb dealers at temples in Tokyo and Kyoto) for noodle soups and yakitori. This version features urfa biber, a sun-dried Turkish chile that is smoky and raisiny and has slow-building heat. There's a pinch of coconut blossom sugar for just enough sweetness to bring out all of the contrasting flavors. I think shichimi is extremely versatile; I use it in just about any dish where I would use black pepper.

NOTE: Ground sansho and dried shredded nori are available at Japanese markets as well as online. Coconut blossom sugar is available in some grocery stores and online; light brown or muscovado sugar can be substituted.

MAKES ABOUT ⅓ CUP [30 G]

2 Tbsp black or white sesame seeds

3 Tbsp dried shredded nori

2 Tbsp dried orange peel

2 Tbsp urfa biber

2 Tbsp Aleppo pepper

1 tsp ground sansho

¼ tsp coconut blossom sugar

¼ tsp salt

Toast the sesame seeds in a small, dry frying pan over medium heat, stirring frequently, until golden brown and fragrant, 1 to 2 minutes.

Mix the toasted sesame seeds, nori, orange peel, urfa biber, Aleppo pepper, sansho, coconut blossom sugar, and salt in a bowl. Store in a covered container in a cool, dark place for up to 1 month.

Arbol-guajillo furikake

Japanese furikake typically includes dried seaweed mixed with ingredients such as dried bonito and sesame seeds. This spice-and-seed mixture is a cross between Japanese furikake and a Mexican dry salsa of chiles, pumpkin seeds, and sesame seeds. I use it sprinkled over salads, foie gras torchon, pizza, pasta, and omelets, and in sandwiches, vinaigrettes, and rubs.

NOTE: Aonori is ground dried Japanese seaweed and is available at Japanese markets and online.

MAKES ABOUT 1 CUP [210 G]

½ cup [65 g] white sesame seeds
½ cup [60 g] pepitas (hulled pumpkin seeds)
¼ cup [60 ml] avocado or olive oil
1 large garlic clove, sliced
1 or 2 dried arbol chiles, coarsely chopped
3 or 4 dried guajillo chiles, coarsely chopped
Pinch of salt
1 Tbsp aonori

Toast the sesame seeds in a small, dry frying pan over medium heat, stirring frequently, until golden brown and fragrant, about 3 minutes. Remove from the heat, transfer to a bowl, and set aside.

Toast the pepitas in the same frying pan over medium heat, stirring occasionally, until golden brown and fragrant, 4 to 5 minutes. Remove from the heat, transfer to the bowl with the sesame seeds, and set aside.

Heat the oil in the same frying pan over medium heat until hot and shimmering. Add the garlic and sauté, stirring constantly, until golden brown and fragrant, 30 to 40 seconds. Add the arbol and guajillo chiles and toast until fragrant, 30 to 40 seconds. Add the toasted sesame seeds, pumpkin seeds, salt, and aonori, and stir to combine. Remove from the heat.

Transfer the mixture to a food processor and pulse a few times to coarsely chop the pumpkin seeds and chiles. You can also chop the mixture with a knife. Store in a covered container in the refrigerator for up to 1 week.

Coffee-spice rub

My great-grandparents, Papa and Mama Grande, started a small chain of Centeno Supermarkets in San Antonio (later taken over by a big chain). When I was a kid, my dad, who was trained as a butcher at the stores, would bring home all of his favorite cuts of meat—hanger steaks, flat irons, short ribs. Before and during grilling, he basted these with his own barbecue mop. The most important ingredient was coffee. I think it's because coffee somehow makes meat taste more meaty. This dry rub—which is great for oily fish like yellowtail collar or mackerel as well as meats such as steaks, roasts, and lamb—is inspired by his coffee mop. I've added a lot of spices: mustard powder, chili powder, smoked paprika, ginger, and Aleppo pepper. These are a good match for bitter, earthy coffee and make this an intense, flavor-concentrated rub.

NOTE: You can substitute Aleppo pepper with any coarsely ground, mildly spicy dried chile, such as New Mexico chiles, urfa biber, or cascabel.

MAKES ABOUT 1¾ CUPS [260 G]

¼ cup [30 g] coffee beans, finely ground

¼ cup [35 g] smoked paprika

¼ cup [50 g] firmly packed dark brown sugar

¼ cup [40 g] salt

¼ cup [35 g] freshly ground black pepper

¼ cup [35 g] Aleppo pepper

1 Tbsp yellow mustard powder

1 Tbsp ground ginger

1 Tbsp chili powder

Thoroughly mix the coffee, smoked paprika, brown sugar, salt, black pepper, Aleppo pepper, mustard powder, ginger, and chili powder in a bowl. Store in an airtight container or sealed plastic storage bag in the freezer for up to 3 months.

Harrough

I've been calling this spice mixture "harrough" for so long that I came to think of it as a real word. But I made it up. Pronounced *hah-roo,* it has all the flavors of the North African condiment harissa, but with several spices beyond the traditional cumin, caraway, and chiles—and it's superconcentrated into a thick paste. It's meant to be used as an extra punch of flavor, stirred into soups, braises, dressings, sauces, and other spice blends. I first made it at Bäco Mercat as an addition to the noodle soup called bäzole, which is a cross between Mexican pozole and Japanese ramen. It makes for a deep, rich, spicy broth. Every few months, I'd make a huge batch, filling a dozen sheet trays with dried chiles, my eyes watering like crazy. But it's worth braving the capsaicinoids (wear gloves!) because this dry harissa transforms everything, and just a little goes a long, long way.

NOTE: Ground rosebud powder is available at Middle Eastern markets and online.

MAKES ABOUT ¾ CUP [70 G]

2 Tbsp caraway seeds

1 Tbsp cumin seeds

½ Tbsp coriander seeds

½ Tbsp fennel seeds

½ tsp cardamom seeds

4 whole cloves

12 dried chipotle chiles

8 dried California or New Mexico chiles

¼ cup [7 g] dried arbol chiles

2 Tbsp finely grated red onion

⅛ tsp ground cinnamon

¼ tsp ground ginger

¼ tsp ground turmeric

¼ tsp cayenne pepper

¼ tsp salt

⅛ tsp freshly ground black pepper

3 Tbsp olive oil

½ tsp rosebud powder

cont'd

Toast the caraway, cumin, coriander, fennel, cardamom, and cloves in a small, dry frying pan over medium heat, stirring occasionally, until fragrant, 3 to 4 minutes. Remove from the heat.

Grind the spices to a fine powder in a spice grinder or using a mortar and pestle. Sift through a fine-mesh strainer into a large bowl and discard any hulls or stems. Set aside.

Heat the oven to 325°F [165°C]. Wearing gloves, remove and discard the stems and seeds from the dried chiles. Tear the chipotle and California chiles into large pieces. Spread them and the arbol chiles in a single layer on a baking sheet and place on a middle rack in the oven. Toast until fragrant, 10 to 12 minutes. Set aside to cool slightly.

Put the chiles in a blender or food processor (in batches, if necessary) and blend or process on medium speed until finely ground. Be careful when blending the chiles because capsaicin molecules released into the air can also cause coughing. Transfer the chiles to the bowl with the spices. Add the onion, cinnamon, ginger, turmeric, cayenne, salt, black pepper, olive oil, and rosebud powder and mix thoroughly with gloved hands until you have a very thick paste. Store in a covered jar in the refrigerator for up to 3 months, or in a sealed plastic storage bag in the freezer for up to 3 months (or up to 6 months if you can vacuum seal it).

Dukkah many ways

The Egyptian seasoning dukkah typically includes nuts, coriander, cumin, and sesame seeds. But each Egyptian kitchen or spice vendor has its own variation. The word *dukkah* comes from the Arabic for "to pound," because that's how dukkah is made—by crushing the ingredients. The best texture comes from making it with a mortar and pestle. It should be a little chunky, somewhere between a powder and a nut mix that you can snack on from your hand. Traditionally, it's eaten with warm flatbread that is first dipped in olive oil. Use it on roast chicken and lamb, scrambled or soft-boiled eggs, hummus, salads, and raw vegetables, and in soups and sauces. I've sprinkled it on cavatelli with pork sugo, peaches and burrata, seared foie gras, even ice cream. I make it with various combinations of ingredients, including a couple of breakfast versions for eating on top of porridge or homemade yogurt (page 90).

Toasting seeds

Toast seeds of similar size and density together. I often toast cumin, coriander, and cardamom seeds in the same pan, for example. But sesame seeds are much smaller than, say, fennel seeds. If heated together, the sesame seeds will have been scorched by the time the fennel seeds are toasted. Toast coconut flakes in the same way.

The mortar and pestle

Restaurants are filled with all kinds of technology devoted to grinding, crushing, and puréeing ingredients: food processors, Vitamix blenders, Thermomixes, Robot Coupes. But I find myself returning to the mortar and pestle as much as possible, for harissa (page 62) and muhammara (page 59), as well as for dukkah. For dukkah, I crush the ingredients in stages—the spices, the seeds, the nuts—so that I have as much control as possible over the size of the grind; nothing should be too finely powdered.

NOTE: Harrough (page 42) also can be substituted with urfa biber or Aleppo pepper.

MAKES ½ TO ¾ CUP [85 TO 110 G]

cont'd

Virginia peanut and coriander dukkah

NOTE: I like using Virginia peanuts because of their large size, preferably with their skins on for extra flavor, texture, and color. They are available in some specialty stores and online.

½ cup [70 g] skin-on roasted salted Virginia peanuts
1 Tbsp white sesame seeds
1 Tbsp coriander seeds
½ Tbsp cumin seeds
½ tsp caraway seeds
¼ tsp flaky sea salt
¼ tsp freshly ground black pepper
½ tsp harrough (page 42) or red pepper flakes

Lightly crush the peanuts with a mortar and pestle until just broken up. Put them in a small bowl and set aside.

Toast the sesame seeds in a small, dry frying pan over medium heat, stirring frequently, until golden brown and fragrant, 1 to 2 minutes. Add the sesame seeds to the bowl with the peanuts and set aside.

Toast the coriander, cumin, and caraway in the same frying pan over medium heat, stirring occasionally, until fragrant, about 3 minutes. Crush the seed mixture and salt using a mortar and pestle until just broken up. Add this to the peanuts, along with the black pepper and harrough. Stir to blend. Store in a covered container in a cool, dark place for up to 1 month.

Hazelnut and fennel dukkah

½ cup [70 g] hazelnuts

1 Tbsp white sesame seeds

1 Tbsp coriander seeds

½ tsp cumin seeds

1½ Tbsp fennel seeds

½ tsp flaky sea salt

¼ tsp freshly ground black pepper

½ tsp harrough (page 42) or red pepper flakes

1 Tbsp extra-virgin olive oil

Heat the oven to 350°F [180°C]. Spread the nuts in a single layer on a baking sheet and place on a middle rack in the oven. Roast, stirring the nuts once for even cooking, until toasty and fragrant, about 15 minutes. Cool slightly, then lightly crush the nuts using a mortar and pestle until just broken up. Put them in a small bowl and set aside.

Toast the sesame seeds in a small, dry frying pan over medium heat, stirring frequently, until golden brown and fragrant, 1 to 2 minutes. Add the sesame seeds to the bowl with the hazelnuts and set aside.

Toast the coriander, cumin, and fennel seeds in the same frying pan over medium heat, stirring occasionally, until fragrant, about 3 minutes. Crush the seed mixture and salt using a mortar and pestle until just broken up. Add this to the hazelnuts, along with the black pepper, harrough, and olive oil. Stir to blend. Store in a covered container in a cool, dark place for up to 1 month.

Almond and sumac dukkah

½ cup [70 g] whole almonds
1 Tbsp white sesame seeds
1 Tbsp coriander seeds
½ Tbsp cumin seeds
¼ tsp cubeb pepper
½ tsp flaky sea salt
½ Tbsp ground sumac
¼ tsp grated lemon zest
½ Tbsp olive oil

Heat the oven to 350°F [180°C]. Spread the almonds in a single layer on a baking sheet and place on a middle rack in the oven. Roast, stirring the almonds once for even cooking, until toasty and fragrant, about 7 minutes. Cool slightly. Lightly crush the almonds using a mortar and pestle until just broken up. Put them in a small bowl and set aside.

Toast the sesame seeds in a small, dry frying pan over medium heat, stirring frequently, until golden brown and fragrant, 1 to 2 minutes. Add the sesame seeds to the bowl with the almonds and set aside.

Toast the coriander, cumin, and cubeb pepper in the same frying pan over medium heat, stirring occasionally, until fragrant, about 3 minutes. Crush the seed and pepper mixture and the salt using a mortar and pestle until just broken up. Add this to the almonds, along with the sumac, lemon zest, and olive oil. Stir to blend. Store in a covered container in a cool, dark place for up to 1 month.

Marcona almond, coconut, and rosebud breakfast dukkah

NOTE: Dried rosebuds are available at Middle Eastern markets and spice shops as well as online. You can substitute one or two dried lavender buds for the rosebud. Use just one bud if you would like a less floral dukkah.

½ cup [70 g] roasted salted Marcona almonds
1 Tbsp white sesame seeds
3 Tbsp unsweetened shredded coconut
1 Tbsp coriander seeds
⅛ tsp cardamom seeds
¼ tsp flaky sea salt
1 or 2 dried rosebuds

Lightly crush the Marcona almonds using a mortar and pestle until just broken up. Put them in a small bowl and set aside.

Toast the sesame seeds in a small, dry frying pan over medium heat, stirring frequently, until golden brown and fragrant, 1 to 2 minutes. Add the sesame seeds to the bowl with the almonds and set aside. Toast the coconut in the same pan over medium heat, stirring occasionally, until golden brown and fragrant, about 4 minutes. Add the coconut to the bowl with the almonds and sesame seeds and set aside.

Toast the coriander and cardamom seeds in the same frying pan over medium heat, stirring frequently, until fragrant, about 3 minutes. Crush the seed mixture, sea salt, and rosebuds using a mortar and pestle until just broken up. Add this to the almond mixture. Stir to blend. Store in a covered container in a cool, dark place for up to 1 month.

Cashew and coconut breakfast dukkah

½ cup [70 g] whole cashews or pecan halves

1 Tbsp white sesame seeds

3 Tbsp unsweetened shredded coconut

1½ Tbsp pepitas (hulled pumpkin seeds)

½ Tbsp cumin seeds

½ Tbsp coriander seeds

½ tsp flaky sea salt

¼ tsp freshly ground black pepper

Heat the oven to 350°F [180°C]. Spread the cashews in a single layer on a baking sheet and place on a middle rack in the oven. Roast, stirring the nuts once for even cooking, until toasty and fragrant, about 7 minutes. Cool slightly. Lightly crush the nuts using a mortar and pestle until just broken up. Put them in a small bowl and set aside.

Toast the sesame seeds in a small, dry frying pan over medium heat, stirring frequently, until golden brown and fragrant, 1 to 2 minutes. Add the sesame seeds to the bowl with the cashews and set aside. Toast the coconut in the same pan over medium heat, stirring occasionally, until golden brown and fragrant, about 4 minutes. Add the coconut to the bowl with the nuts and set aside.

Toast the pumpkin seeds, cumin, and coriander in the same frying pan over medium heat, stirring occasionally, until fragrant, about 3 minutes. Crush the seed mixture and salt using a mortar and pestle until just broken up. Add this and the black pepper to the nut mixture. Stir to blend. Store in a covered container in a cool, dark place for up to 1 month.

More ways to dukkah

Dukkah is popular far beyond Egypt—you can't throw a pistachio without hitting it on a restaurant menu. But I usually see recipes that show just one particular way to make it. Dukkah invites experimentation in combining a lot of flavors—savory, spicy, salty, tart, sweet, peppery—and textures, too. Use almost any kind of nut, with a combination of a little cumin, coriander, and other spices, seeds, cereals, and flaky sea salt.

Nuts

ALMONDS

PISTACHIOS

HAZELNUTS

PECANS

CASHEWS

PEANUTS

MARCONA ALMONDS

BRAZIL NUTS

WALNUTS

PINE NUTS

Spices and herbs

FLAKY SEA SALT

TELLICHERRY BLACK PEPPERCORNS

WHITE PEPPERCORNS

CAYENNE

GROUND TURMERIC

RED PEPPER FLAKES

ZA'ATAR

DRIED MINT

DRIED FENUGREEK LEAVES

GROUND CINNAMON

PIMENT D'ESPELETTE

Seeds

CORIANDER

WHITE CUMIN

BLACK CUMIN

WHITE SESAME

BLACK SESAME

FENNEL

FENUGREEK

NIGELLA

GRAINS OF PARADISE

PEPITAS (HULLED PUMPKIN SEEDS)

SUNFLOWER SEEDS

POPPY SEEDS

HEMPSEEDS

Other

UNSWEETENED SHREDDED COCONUT

LIGHT BROWN SUGAR

MUSCOVADO SUGAR

FINELY GROUND ESPRESSO

CACAO NIBS

GRATED ORANGE ZEST

GRATED LEMON ZEST

PUFFED QUINOA

DRIED SHALLOTS

MILLET

DRIED EDIBLE FLOWERS SUCH AS LAVENDER BUDS
OR ROSE PETALS

Caraway croutons

Crunchy croutons come in handy, and these are seasoned with caraway, thyme, garlic, and Pecorino cheese. The caraway seeds can be ground without first toasting them; they get toasty in the oven with the croutons.

MAKES ABOUT 3 CUPS [140 G]

2 Tbsp butter

2 Tbsp olive oil

10 sprigs thyme, tied with kitchen string

1 garlic clove, crushed

2 tsp caraway seeds, coarsely ground

8 oz [230 g] country white bread, crust removed and torn into 1-in [2.5-cm] pieces

¼ cup [30 g] grated Pecorino cheese

½ tsp salt

⅛ tsp freshly ground black pepper

Heat the oven to 400°F [200°C].

Heat the butter, oil, thyme, garlic, and caraway in a large frying pan over medium-high heat. When the butter begins to foam, add all of the bread and toast, stirring frequently, until lightly browned, 3 to 4 minutes. Transfer the contents of the frying pan to a parchment paper–lined baking sheet. Sprinkle the Pecorino, salt, and pepper evenly over the toasted bread.

Bake until crunchy throughout and dark golden brown, about 15 minutes, rotating the baking sheet and stirring the croutons once during cooking. Remove from the oven and cool completely. Discard the thyme sprigs and garlic clove. Store in an airtight container at room temperature for up to 3 days.

VARIATION

Caraway bread crumbs: To make bread crumbs, pulse the croutons in a food processor 10 to 12 times until coarsely ground. MAKES 2 CUPS [130 G]

Bacon bread crumb persillade

Persillade is parsley (the French for parsley is *persil*) with seasonings such as garlic, other herbs, oil, and vinegar. This one is seasoned with bacon and caraway bread crumbs. Use it as a garnish for salads, soups, rice dishes, pasta, vegetables—just about anywhere you would otherwise use bread crumbs.

MAKES ABOUT ½ CUP [80 G]

2½ slices bacon, cut into ½-in [12-mm] pieces
½ cup [40 g] caraway croutons (facing page)
½ cup [7 g] fresh parsley leaves, finely chopped
Pinch of salt
Fresh black pepper

Put the bacon in a frying pan over medium-high heat and cook, stirring occasionally, until browned and crispy, about 7 minutes. Transfer the bacon with a slotted spoon to a paper towel–lined plate. Cool completely.

In a food processor, pulse the croutons 10 to 12 times until finely chopped. Transfer to a medium bowl. Finely chop the cooled bacon with a sharp knife. Add the bacon and parsley to the bowl with the bread crumbs. Add the salt and a couple of grinds of black pepper and stir until combined. The persillade is best the day it's made. If not using right away, store in an airtight container in the refrigerator for up to 3 days; rewarm in the oven at 300°F [150°C] for 10 minutes.

Walnut-miso bagna cauda

This is a version of the warm Piedmontese dip of anchovy, garlic, butter, and olive oil. Here it's enriched with white miso and sesame paste instead of butter and gets a little spicy heat from urfa biber. Red-skinned walnuts are available in the fall at farmers' markets in California and have an especially beautiful color; you can substitute other walnuts. Serve warm or hot with vegetables, roasted or fried potatoes, steaks, roasts, or just good bread.

NOTE: You can substitute urfa biber with any coarsely ground, dried, mildly spicy chile, such as New Mexico chile, Aleppo pepper, or cascabel. I use Japanese sesame paste, labeled atari goma, which can be found at Japanese markets and online. It can be substituted with high-quality unsalted tahini.

MAKES ABOUT 1½ CUPS [260 G]

1 garlic clove

2 anchovy fillets

½ cup [120 ml] olive oil

1 cup [120 g] walnuts, preferably red walnuts, coarsely chopped

1 Tbsp white miso

1 Tbsp sesame paste

Juice of 1 lemon

1 tsp urfa biber

Mash the garlic and anchovies to a coarse paste with a mortar and pestle. Transfer to a small saucepan and add the oil. Heat the mixture over medium-low heat, stirring occasionally, until the garlic is aromatic and golden, about 1 minute. Add the walnuts, stirring occasionally, and cook until toasted, about 1 minute. Stir in the miso, then immediately remove from the heat.

Stir in the sesame paste, lemon juice, and urfa biber. The bagna cauda is best used within a day or two. If not using right away, store in a covered container in the refrigerator for up to 1 day; rewarm in a small pan over medium heat.

Sunflower-miso tahini

This version of rich, creamy tahini includes both toasted sunflower and sesame seeds, along with a little Japanese white miso. The through line here is the subtle sweetness of the seeds and miso. But the fermented barley, rice, and soybeans of the miso also make it especially savory. Smear it on flatbread such as Bäco bread (page 176) or toast, make a dressing for a leafy salad, add it to sauces (such as for sesame noodles), or mix it into yogurt with granola and honey. At Bäco Mercat, it gets swirled into a dish of hand-milled grits with pickled serrano chiles and blistered tomatoes (page 238).

MAKES ABOUT 1½ CUPS [360 G]

1 cup [130 g] sunflower seeds
1 cup [120 g] white sesame seeds
1½ Tbsp white miso
½ tsp sugar
¾ cup [180 ml] avocado or olive oil

Toast the sunflower seeds in a small, dry frying pan over medium heat, stirring frequently, until golden brown and fragrant, 4 to 5 minutes. Remove from the heat, transfer the sunflower seeds to a bowl, and set aside.

Toast the sesame seeds in the same frying pan over medium heat, stirring frequently, until golden brown and fragrant, 3 to 4 minutes. Remove from the heat.

Put the sunflower seeds and sesame seeds in a food processor and blend to a coarse, crumbly paste. Add the miso and sugar and process until well combined. With the processor running, slowly pour in the oil and process until the mixture is a smooth paste, stopping and scraping down the sides if necessary. Store in a lidded jar in the refrigerator for up to 1 month.

Muhammara

The word *muhammara* means "brick colored" in Arabic, a reference to the color of this walnut-chile paste. It is nutty, tangy, spicy, pleasantly bitter, and slightly sweet, with a satisfying texture that comes not just from toasted walnuts but also bread crumbs, though I sometimes use panko or even crumbled crackers. Aleppo pepper lends its oily, fruity, and salty flavor. It can be substituted with urfa biber, ground dried cascabel, ground ancho chile, or piment d'Espelette. I think it's the bright-tart-sweet-rich pomegranate molasses that makes muhammara so addictive. I sometimes add the finely chopped leaves of half a bunch of fresh cilantro or mint for herbal freshness.

MAKES 1 CUP [250 G]

1 cup [120 g] whole walnuts

1 tsp cumin seeds

1 garlic clove

1 Thai chile or 1 tsp red pepper flakes or Aleppo pepper

1 tsp flaky sea salt

4 jarred piquillo peppers

2 Tbsp pomegranate and beet molasses (page 32) or bottled pomegranate molasses

Juice of ½ lemon

1 Tbsp extra-virgin olive oil

1 tsp sherry vinegar

1 tsp Aleppo pepper

2 Tbsp dried bread crumbs or panko (optional)

Heat the oven to 350°F [180°C]. Spread the walnuts in a single layer on a baking sheet and place on a middle rack in the oven. Roast, stirring the nuts once for even cooking, until toasty and fragrant, 12 to 15 minutes. Set aside to cool.

Meanwhile, toast the cumin seeds in a small, dry frying pan over medium heat, stirring occasionally, until fragrant, about 1 minute. Remove from the heat. Grind to a fine powder with a mortar and pestle. Add the garlic, Thai chile, and salt and crush with the pestle. Add the piquillo peppers and walnuts and grind to a coarse paste.

Stir in the pomegranate and beet molasses, lemon juice, oil, vinegar, Aleppo pepper, and bread crumbs (if using). Use immediately or store in a covered container in the refrigerator for up to 3 days.

Mortar-and-pestle romesco

I had just started working for David Kinch, now the Michelin three-star chef of Manresa in Los Gatos, California, when he asked me if I'd ever made romesco. As someone who grew up in Texas and worked mostly in French kitchens in New York, I hadn't. So he made it, and when I tasted it, it blew me away—I think this is how a lot of people probably feel when they try romesco for the first time. But his romesco was a revelation and would be the basis for the way I started putting flavors together. The peppers, vinegar, smokiness, nuttiness, umami, salt—everything was colliding and balanced at the same time. This is how I currently make romesco: with both hazelnuts and almonds, both lemon juice and sherry vinegar, a handful of piquillo peppers, harrough for depth, and an anchovy fillet or two, as the mood strikes, for even more umami. Use a mortar and pestle for a not-too-smooth texture.

NOTE: Harrough can be substituted with urfa biber or red pepper flakes.

MAKES ABOUT 1½ CUPS [310 G]

½ cup [70 g] hazelnuts
½ cup [70 g] whole almonds
6 jarred piquillo peppers
1 anchovy fillet
2 garlic cloves
1 tsp flaky sea salt
2 Tbsp olive oil
1 Tbsp sherry vinegar
Grated zest and juice of ½ lemon
½ Tbsp smoked paprika
½ tsp harrough (page 42)

Heat the oven to 350°F [180°C]. Spread the hazelnuts and almonds in a single layer on a baking sheet and place on a middle rack in the oven. Roast, stirring the nuts once for even cooking, until toasty and fragrant, about 15 minutes. Set aside to cool.

Put the piquillo peppers, anchovy, garlic, and salt in a mortar and grind with a pestle until the mixture is a coarse paste. Add the hazelnuts and almonds and crush them lightly. Stir in the oil, vinegar, lemon zest, lemon juice, paprika, and harrough. Use immediately or store in a covered container in the refrigerator for up to 5 days.

Mortar-and-pestle harissa

Harissa has mythic status in my mind. I love the color, texture, and taste of of this rich paste—ultra-red, thick, and spicy—spicy in the sense that it has a lot of spices and plenty of chile heat. I use, for the most part, some combination of the dried chiles guajillo, New Mexican, and/or ancho because they're closest to the Tunisian peppers Gabès and Nabeul. This rustic version is prepared with a mortar and pestle. You could also use a food processor; grind the toasted cumin and caraway before blending the harissa to a smooth paste.

NOTE: Harrough also can be substituted with red pepper flakes, or use 1 or 2 additional dried arbol chiles. This recipe can be halved if your mortar is small.

MAKES ABOUT 2 CUPS [350 G]

6 dried guajillo chiles
4 dried arbol chiles
2 dried ancho chiles
4 tsp caraway seeds
4 tsp cumin seeds
2 garlic cloves, peeled
2 tsp flaky sea salt
4 tsp smoked paprika
8 jarred piquillo peppers
2 tsp harrough (page 42) or urfa biber
4 tsp olive oil
4 tsp sherry vinegar

Bring a kettle of water to a boil. Put the guajillo, arbol, and ancho chiles in a medium bowl and pour boiling water over them. Rehydrate until softened, about 15 minutes.

Meanwhile, toast the caraway and cumin seeds in a small, dry frying pan over medium heat, stirring occasionally, until fragrant, 2 to 3 minutes. Grind to a coarse powder with a mortar and pestle. Add the garlic and salt and grind to a coarse paste.

Thoroughly drain the rehydrated chiles and, wearing gloves, remove and discard the stems and seeds. Add them to the mortar along with the paprika, piquillo peppers, and harrough. Grind with the pestle to blend with the garlic mixture.

Stir in the oil and vinegar until combined. Use immediately or store in a covered container in the refrigerator for up to 1 week.

Salbitxada

I remember buying a secondhand copy of *Culinaria Spain*, a tome devoted to regional Spanish cooking, and the book was transporting. I read about sauces like salbitxada—tomatoes, almonds, garlic, and chiles, traditionally served with grilled calçots, the fat green onions of spring and summer—and was inspired to make my own version. Mine is probably a cross between salbitxada, picada (roasted nuts, garlic, parsley, and olive oil), and Mexican pico de gallo. This salbitxada includes hand-chopped almonds, cherry tomatoes, and parsley, with a glug of good oil and sherry vinegar, some lemon zest, garlic, and a little habanero. It's not the salbitxada I would finally try in Catalonia, which is a thinner purée made with skinned tomatoes. But I have stuck to this version because I like the texture so much.

MAKES ABOUT 2 CUPS [300 G]

¼ cup [35 g] whole almonds

20 cherry or grape tomatoes, halved

1 bunch parsley, leaves only, finely chopped

¼ cup [60 ml] olive oil

2 Tbsp sherry vinegar

Grated zest of ½ lemon

½ tsp salt

1 garlic clove

½ habanero chile or 1 tsp red pepper flakes

Heat the oven to 350°F [180°C]. Spread the almonds in a single layer in an oven-safe pan and place on a middle rack in the oven. Roast, stirring the nuts once for even cooking, until toasty and fragrant, about 10 minutes. Set aside to cool.

Put the tomatoes, parsley, olive oil, sherry vinegar, lemon zest, and salt in a large bowl. Coarsely chop the almonds and add them to the tomato mixture. Grate the garlic into the bowl using a zester, then do the same with the habanero. Stir to combine. The salbitxada is best the day it's made. If not using right away, store in a covered container in the refrigerator for up to 1 day.

Adjika vinaigrette

I love the flavors of adjika, the traditional spicy pepper dip of Abkhazia and Georgia, made with spicy red peppers, garlic, coriander seeds, dried fenugreek, and fresh herbs. The homemade versions sold in markets across the isthmus that separates the Black and Caspian seas vary from vendor to vendor. I have my own version, too, which includes celery, a little fresh Thai chile, piquillo peppers, and Calabrian chiles—the latter for their smokiness. I loosely refer to this recipe as a vinaigrette. It's prepared in much the same way as salsa verde (page 70), by finely chopping the ingredients with a very sharp knife and mixing them with oil and vinegar. It's simultaneously refreshing (thanks to a lot of celery and cilantro), pungent, and spicy. Use it for steaks, roast chicken, cooked fish or crudo, salads, and steamed or grilled vegetables.

MAKES ABOUT ½ CUP [110 G]

¾ tsp coriander seeds
1 Tbsp dried fenugreek leaves
1 Tbsp fresh oregano leaves
8 fresh basil leaves
¼ cup [4 g] fresh cilantro leaves
¼ cup [4 g] celery leaves
1 small garlic clove
1 Thai chile, seeded
1 jarred piquillo pepper
3 jarred Calabrian chiles
¼ cup [60 ml] olive oil
1 Tbsp sherry vinegar
Salt

Toast the coriander seeds in a small, dry frying pan over medium heat, stirring occasionally, until fragrant, about 2 minutes. Grind to a fine powder in a spice grinder or with a mortar and pestle. Put the ground coriander in a medium bowl and set aside.

One ingredient at a time, finely chop the fenugreek, oregano, basil, cilantro, celery leaves, and garlic, adding them to the bowl as you go. Wearing gloves, finely chop the Thai chile, piquillo pepper, and Calabrian chiles and add to the bowl.

Gently stir in the olive oil and sherry vinegar. The jarred peppers can be fairly salty, so taste the vinaigrette and season with salt as needed. Store in a covered container in the refrigerator for up to 3 days.

Salmorejo

Salmorejo is another Spanish staple that took hold in my imagination. Made from ground tomatoes, garlic, bread, and oil, it's an Andalusian purée traditionally served cold like gazpacho, but thicker and creamier. Parents would send their kids to school with a concentrate of salmorejo, and at lunch on a warm summer day, they'd just add water for a delicious chilled soup, maybe garnished with a little chopped ham or shrimp or boiled egg. The acidity in the vinegar and tomatoes (I also use lemon juice) makes it especially refreshing. The key here is ripe summer tomatoes. I use my version of salmorejo like a sauce, intensified with chile and harrough. It's smeared on sandwiches and toast, or served with roasted fish or vegetable fritters or baked eggs. It works just as well without the bread crumbs, thinned out with a little extra olive oil into a tomato sauce or vinaigrette.

NOTE: Harrough also can be substituted with the Turkish ground chile urfa biber or red pepper flakes.

MAKES 2 CUPS [480 G]

12 ripe tomatoes
1 bunch parsley, leaves only, chopped
Juice of 1 lemon
1 Tbsp sherry vinegar
1 tsp salt
Fresh black pepper
2 garlic cloves
½ habanero chile
1 tsp harrough (page 42, optional)
¾ cup [75 g] caraway bread crumbs (page 54)

Grate the tomatoes on the medium holes of a box grater into a large bowl and discard the skins. Add the parsley, lemon juice, sherry vinegar, salt, and a few grinds of black pepper.

Grate the garlic cloves into the bowl using a zester, then do the same with the habanero. Stir to combine. Stir in the harrough (if using). Gently stir in the bread crumbs just before serving.

If not using right away, keep the bread crumbs separate and store the salmorejo in a covered container in the refrigerator for up to 3 days.

Fenugreek-chipotle tomato sauce

Dried fenugreek leaves (sometimes labeled *kasoori methi* in Indian markets) are as flavorful as fresh leaves and remind me of fennel and celery, a little bitter but also a little sweet. I've always loved fenugreek leaves in the Persian stew *ghormeh sabzi* and in Indian dals. I've come to think of it as the oregano of South Asia, partly because it does such a good job of bringing out the savory notes of tomatoes, so I incorporated some into an all-purpose tomato sauce. The leaves are added at the last minute so that their flavor is more pronounced. Use this tomato sauce for vegetables, pastas, and stews.

MAKES ABOUT 2 CUPS [650 G]

3 Tbsp olive oil
8 garlic cloves, sliced
One 28-oz [794-g] can whole tomatoes, crushed by hand, with their juice
2 chipotle chiles with adobo sauce, seeded and minced
1 Tbsp dark brown sugar
1 Tbsp sherry vinegar
¼ tsp salt
½ cup [12 g] fresh basil leaves
1 Tbsp dried fenugreek leaves

Heat the olive oil in a medium saucepan over medium heat until hot and shimmering. Add the garlic, and cook, stirring frequently, until sizzling and fragrant, about 1 minute; it shouldn't brown.

Add the tomatoes with their juice, chipotle chiles, brown sugar, sherry vinegar, and salt. Turn the heat to medium-high and bring the sauce to a boil. Lower the heat, partially cover, and gently simmer, stirring occasionally, until the sauce has reduced by about a third, 20 to 25 minutes.

Remove from the heat. Stir in the basil. Sprinkle in the fenugreek leaves, slightly crushing them between your fingers as you drop them into the sauce, then stir to combine. Use immediately or store in a covered container in the refrigerator for up to 3 days.

Chermou-lata

This sauce is inspired by all the versions of North African chermoula I've ever come across, melded with Italian gremolata. Chermoula is typically a purée of parsley, cilantro, cumin, coriander, olive oil, and lemon juice. There are regional varieties, with ingredients that include cloves, cinnamon, preserved lemons, chiles, onion, paprika, saffron, and even grapes. Gremolata, on the other hand, is pretty much always just three ingredients—chopped parsley, garlic, and lemon zest—and maybe occasionally toasted pine nuts, or horse-radish instead of garlic. I like gremolata for its simplicity and freshness, and I like chermoula for its punch and the fact that it varies so much from cook to cook. So here's my combination of the two.

NOTE: Harrough also can be substituted with urfa biber or Aleppo pepper.

MAKES ABOUT 1½ CUPS [300 G]

¼ cup [35 g] pine nuts
½ tsp cumin seeds
½ tsp coriander seeds
1 bunch cilantro, leaves only
1 bunch parsley, leaves only
Grated zest of 3 oranges
Grated zest of 3 lemons
¼ cup [60 ml] fresh lemon juice
1 tsp harrough (page 42) or red pepper flakes
½ cup [120 ml] olive oil
½ tsp ground sumac
2 garlic cloves, peeled

Toast the pine nuts in a small, dry frying pan over medium heat, stirring frequently, until browned, about 2 minutes. Remove from the heat, transfer to a small bowl, and set aside.

Toast the cumin and coriander seeds in the same frying pan over medium heat, stirring occasionally, until fragrant, about 1 minute. Grind the spices to a fine powder in a spice grinder or with a mortar and pestle. Set aside.

Finely chop the cilantro and parsley leaves. Put them in a large bowl and add the orange zest, lemon zest, lemon juice, harrough, olive oil, toasted pine nuts, cumin and coriander, and the sumac. Grate the garlic cloves into the bowl using a zester. Stir to combine. Use immediately or store in a covered container in the refrigerator for up to 2 days.

VARIATION
Chermou-lata butter

½ cup [115 g] butter, at room temperature
2 Tbsp chermou-lata (see recipe)

Put the butter and chermou-lata in a large bowl and beat together with an electric mixer or by hand with a wooden spoon until well combined. Lay a piece of plastic wrap on a flat surface. Gather the butter with a spatula and scoop it onto the center of the plastic wrap. Roll the plastic wrap around the butter, forming a log. Twist the ends of the plastic wrap and put the butter in the refrigerator for about 2 hours to set. (Alternatively, spoon the butter into an airtight container for storage.) Store in the refrigerator for up to 3 days. Or wrap the log in both plastic wrap and aluminum foil and store in the freezer for up to 2 months.

Mint and fines herbes salsa verde

Salsa verde, a condiment of fresh herbs that's hundreds if not thousands of years old, is the ubiquitous green sauce of so many cultures. First brought to Italy from Western Asia by Roman soldiers, Italian salsa verde is a sauce of olive oil, chopped parsley, lemon zest, garlic, and capers. But adding other fresh, soft herbs only enhances it. I use a base of fines herbes—the French combination of parsley, chives, tarragon, and chervil—along with dill and mint. I like the anise undertones of tarragon and the citrusy spark in dill. Playing around with what you have is encouraged. I also add Calabrian chiles. Salsa verde can be used as a vinaigrette for salad, spooned over seared steaks, lengua, grilled fish and shrimp, or cured meats such as coppa di testa. Use it as a dip for crudités, smear it onto focaccia, drizzle it over some scrambled eggs. The important thing here is to use a very sharp knife for the best texture and flavor—a dull knife will bruise your herbs.

NOTE: I also use this salsa verde to make tabbouleh. Reduce the amount of oil to ⅓ cup [80 ml] and add to cooked bulgur, along with some chopped ripe tomatoes.

MAKES ABOUT 1½ CUPS [250 G]

½ cup [8 g] fresh mint leaves

⅓ cup [5 g] dill fronds

⅓ cup [5 g] fresh parsley leaves

⅓ cup [4 g] fresh chervil leaves

2 Tbsp fresh tarragon leaves

½ bunch chives

2 jarred Calabrian chiles

2 Tbsp capers

Grated zest and juice of ½ lemon

½ garlic clove, grated with a zester

½ to ⅔ cup [120 to 160 ml] extra-virgin olive oil, or to taste

¼ tsp salt

Finely chop the mint, dill, parsley, chervil, tarragon, and chives and put them in a medium bowl. Wearing gloves, finely chop the Calabrian chiles and add to the herbs. Stir in the capers, lemon zest, lemon juice, garlic, olive oil, and salt. The salsa verde is best the day it's made. If not using right away, store in a covered container in the refrigerator for up to 3 days.

Lime and fish sauce vinaigrette

Bright, tart lime and the funk of fish sauce give this vinaigrette a lot of punch, which makes it great for just about any vegetable. Prepare this dressing a day in advance and store it in the refrigerator overnight so that the flavors meld.

MAKES ABOUT 1⅓ CUPS [320 ML]

1 cup [240 ml] fresh lime juice

⅓ cup [80 ml] fish sauce

One 3-in [7.5-cm] knob of ginger, peeled, smashed, and cut into chunks

2 garlic cloves, crushed

1 scallion, white and green parts, cut into large pieces

2 serrano chiles, sliced

2 dried arbol chiles

1 tsp freshly ground black pepper

1 tsp coriander seeds

Combine the lime juice, fish sauce, ginger, garlic, scallion, serrano chiles, arbol chiles, and black pepper in a lidded jar or container. Set aside.

Toast the coriander in a small, dry frying pan over medium heat, stirring occasionally, until fragrant, 1 to 2 minutes. Transfer to the jar with the rest of the ingredients. Use a muddler or the end of a wooden spoon to press and twist lightly on the ginger, garlic, scallion, and chiles in the mixture to release their flavors. Cover and refrigerate overnight so that the flavors meld. Strain, discarding the solids, and return the vinaigrette to the jar until ready to use. Store in the refrigerator for up to 1 month.

Juniper-tarragon vinaigrette

In the French kitchens that I have worked in, juniper spice was used to infuse beurre blanc, red wine marinades for game, and jus for roast duck. The herbal, almost medicinal flavor of juniper berries is intriguing: clean, sharp, piney, and slightly sweet, bitter, and tart all at the same time. Its botanical qualities seem like ideal counterparts to some of my other favorite spices and herbs: tarragon, caraway, anise, and coriander seed. Here I use tarragon and fennel to complement the juniper, and lemon zest, lemon juice, and rice vinegar for a hit of brightness. I use this vinaigrette for salads and vegetables and to season hand-cut beef tartare; serve it with some crusty bread and a bone-dry gin martini.

MAKES ¾ CUP [180 ML]

5 dried juniper berries
¼ tsp fennel seeds
2 tsp chopped fresh tarragon
1 garlic clove, peeled
Grated zest and juice of ½ lemon
¼ cup [60 ml] rice vinegar
½ cup [120 ml] olive oil
½ tsp salt
Fresh black pepper

Toast the juniper berries and fennel seeds in a small, dry frying pan over medium heat, stirring occasionally, until fragrant, about 2 minutes. Grind to a fine powder in a spice grinder.

Put the juniper and fennel, tarragon, garlic, lemon zest, lemon juice, rice vinegar, olive oil, salt, and a few grinds of black pepper in a blender and blend on medium to high speed until well combined.

Use immediately or store in a lidded jar in the refrigerator for up to 1 week.

Creamy juniper-tarragon tahini dressing

This is a version of a dressing I once made at a party after I'd forgotten to bring all of the ingredients necessary for a ranch dressing that the host had requested. I improvised by adding tahini and yogurt to the juniper-tarragon vinaigrette, so it was rich and creamy, with bold herbal flavors. Crisis averted.

MAKES ⅔ CUP [160 ML]

¼ cup [60 ml] juniper-tarragon vinaigrette (facing page)
⅓ cup [80 g] crème fraîche (page 94)
1 Tbsp tahini
1 Tbsp Greek yogurt or lebni

Using a wooden spoon, mix the vinaigrette, crème fraîche, tahini, and Greek yogurt in a bowl. This dressing is best the day it's prepared.

"Broken" cipollini-buttermilk dressing

The sweet, browned, slightly smoky caramelized cipollini onions in this dressing play nicely with creamy, tangy buttermilk. They aren't meant to be emulsified but instead suspended in a vinaigrette, so that's why it's called broken. Even though it isn't.

MAKES ABOUT 1½ CUPS [355 ML]

¾ cup plus 3 Tbsp [225 ml] extra-virgin olive oil
5 cipollini onions, cut into fine dice
Salt
¼ cup [60 ml] white wine vinegar
1½ Tbsp buttermilk
1 Tbsp crème fraîche (page 94)
1 Tbsp honey
1 tsp Dijon mustard
Fresh black pepper
2 Tbsp chopped fresh chives

Heat 3 Tbsp [45 ml] of the olive oil in a frying pan over high heat until hot and shimmering. Add the cipollini and a pinch of salt and sauté, stirring frequently, until golden brown and crispy with charred edges, 3 to 4 minutes. Transfer to a paper towel–lined plate. Set aside.

Whisk together the vinegar and ½ tsp salt in a bowl. Whisk in the remaining ¾ cup [180 ml] oil, buttermilk, crème fraîche, honey, mustard, and a few grinds of black pepper until combined.

Fold the cipollini and the chives into the dressing. Use immediately or store in a covered container in the refrigerator for up to 2 days.

bäco

Dashi concentrate

Dashi is one of the cornerstones of Japanese cuisine, an elegantly simple stock traditionally made with just water, kelp, and bonito (or smoked, fermented skipjack). This isn't that dashi; it's an amped-up version that includes both bonito flakes and dried shiitake mushrooms, aromatic onion, garlic, mirin, and rice vinegar, and simmers on the stove until it is reduced by nearly half. I use it a lot for seasoning, especially in a vinaigrette with yuzu juice (facing page) for concentrated umami intensity. It has a lot of oomph. This also can be used in any recipe where you would use dashi, but you might have to adjust for the amount of salt in this version (by reducing the salt in your recipe or adding water to dilute the salty flavor, such as for miso soup).

MAKES A GENEROUS 4 CUPS [950 ML]

8 cups [2 L] water

1 cup [240 ml] sake

¾ cup [35 g] dried shiitake mushrooms

½ yellow onion (from an onion halved crosswise)

½ head garlic (from a head of garlic halved crosswise)

1 piece [20 to 25 g] dried konbu (about 6 by 8 inches [15 by 20 cm])

¼ cup [60 ml] soy sauce

¼ cup [60 ml] mirin

3 Tbsp salt

1 Tbsp rice vinegar

1½ cups [40 g] bonito flakes

Combine the water, sake, mushrooms, onion, garlic, konbu, soy sauce, mirin, salt, and rice vinegar in a stockpot and bring to near boiling over high heat. Turn the heat to medium-low and add the bonito flakes. Simmer for 10 minutes, then carefully remove the konbu with tongs or chopsticks and discard or reserve for another use.

Continue to simmer until the stock has reduced by nearly half, about 45 minutes. Carefully strain the dashi, reserving the liquid and discarding the solids. Use immediately, or store in a covered container in the refrigerator for up to 1 week or freeze for up to 1 month. Dashi normally doesn't freeze well, but this concentrated version does; freeze it in ice cube trays if you want to use a little at a time.

Yuzu-dashi vinaigrette

Tart, floral yuzu meets briny super-dashi in a dressing that can go with grilled fish or crudo, and in pastas, beans, grits, pickles, and salads.

NOTE: High-quality bottled yuzu juice is available at Japanese markets and online.

MAKES A SCANT ²/₃ CUP [150 ML]

¼ cup [60 ml] dashi concentrate (facing page)
¼ cup [60 ml] extra-virgin olive oil
2 Tbsp yuzu juice

Whisk together the dashi concentrate, olive oil, and yuzu juice in a small bowl. Use immediately, or store in a covered container in the refrigerator for up to 2 weeks.

Poblano-feta dip

This creamy dip of roasted poblano chiles and feta cheese is loosely based on kopanisti, a cheese made predominantly on the island of Mykonos. The crumbly, sharp, and spreadable cheese is mixed with red peppers during production. (In Greek, the word *kopanisti* refers to something that has been "beaten.") The cheese inspired a popular dip of the same name, a mixture of feta cheese, red peppers, lemon, herbs, olive oil, and garlic. I use roasted poblano chiles and add a little cumin and a lot of cilantro and mint. It tastes smoky, earthy, spicy, tangy, and fresh. Use it as a spread for sandwiches and burgers, a dip for crudités, a condiment for roasts, or a dressing for salads.

MAKES 1½ CUPS [280 G]

3 poblano chiles
½ tsp cumin seeds
1 cup [14 g] fresh cilantro leaves
1 cup [16 g] fresh mint leaves
1 cup [140 g] crumbled feta
Grated zest and juice of ½ lemon
2 garlic cloves, peeled
1 Tbsp sherry vinegar
½ tsp salt
1 Tbsp to ⅓ cup [15 to 80 ml] water

One at a time, char the poblano chiles by placing them directly over the open flame of a gas stove or grill. Turn them with tongs as they are roasting, until the skins of the chiles are charred and blistered all over, 1 to 2 minutes on each side. While they're hot, place them in a large sealable plastic bag to steam for about 10 minutes. Don't let the chiles steam for too long or they'll start to turn brown. Remove the charred skin, rubbing it off gently with the back of a knife. Cut open one side of each chile and remove and discard the stems, seeds, and ribs. Set aside.

Toast the cumin seeds in a small, dry frying pan over medium heat, stirring occasionally, until fragrant, 1 minute. Remove from the heat.

Put the poblano chiles, cumin, cilantro, mint, feta, lemon zest, lemon juice, garlic, vinegar, and salt in a blender and purée on medium to high speed, adding water a tablespoon at a time, until smooth. Use just enough water to blend the mixture to the consistency of hummus. It shouldn't be too liquidy. Store in a covered container in the refrigerator for up to 2 days.

cont'd

VARIATION

Creamy poblano-feta dressing: For a lighter, creamy-smooth version of poblano-feta dip that also can be used as a dressing, mix equal amounts of poblano-feta dip and crème fraîche (page 94).

Kochkocha

This Ethiopian hot sauce is blazingly spicy and traditionally made with stone-ground chiles mixed with cardamom, onion, ginger, and herbs. The bright green sauce originates from Oromia, a region of rugged mountain ranges and grasslands that cuts a swath across the middle of Ethiopia. Its herb-plus-cardamom flavors remind me of the Yemeni sauce zhoug, but with the addition of a little fresh ginger. Like zhoug, it goes with almost everything—grilled meats, beef or lamb tartare, vegetables, on flatbread—and gives a kick to other sauces and dressings. I use sautéed poblano and serrano chiles (sautéing rounds out the flavor), blended with a lot of cilantro and a little basil, ginger, and vinegar—a fresh combination of heat, acid, and floral and grassy herbs.

NOTE: Ajwain, the fruit of an herb in the parsley family, has a distinct, pungent flavor that's reminiscent of oregano, cumin, and anise. The glossy brown seeds of grains of paradise are peppery and citrusy. Both are available at spice shops and online.

MAKES ABOUT ¾ CUP [180 ML]

¼ cup [55 g] room-temperature ghee (page 86) or ¼ cup [60 ml] olive oil

2 poblano chiles, seeded and chopped

2 serrano chiles, seeded and chopped

1 garlic clove, sliced

1¾ tsp cardamom seeds

½ tsp ajwain

¼ tsp grains of paradise

2 cups [28 g] fresh cilantro leaves

8 large fresh basil leaves

1 Tbsp grated peeled fresh ginger

1½ tsp salt

2 Tbsp distilled white vinegar

Heat the ghee in a frying pan over medium-high heat. When the ghee is hot, add the chiles and garlic and cook, stirring occasionally, just to start the cooking process, about 1 minute. Add the cardamom, ajwain, and grains of paradise and cook until the chiles have just softened (they shouldn't brown), about 1 minute longer. Remove from the heat.

Put the chile mixture, cilantro, basil, ginger, salt, and vinegar in a blender and purée on medium-high speed until smooth. Store in a covered container in the refrigerator for up to 3 days.

Chimichurri

The Argentinian condiment chimichurri—herbaceous, bright with lemon zest and vinegar, and garlicky—is one of my go-to sauces. The team in the kitchen at Bäco Mercat refers to it as a mother sauce; they call it chimi for short because it's used so much. I have added it to everything, including other sauces, doughs for bread and pasta, meatballs, a rub for roasts. It gets smeared on flatbreads, mixed into yogurt for a dressing or dip, and of course served as a condiment for fish, chicken, lamb, or beef. Here I use both spicy, fruity Calabrian chiles along with a fresh Fresno or jalapeño chile and a pinch of pepper flakes too.

MAKES ABOUT 1 CUP [250 G]

1 bunch cilantro, leaves only

½ bunch parsley, leaves only

¼ cup [7 g] fresh oregano leaves

1 garlic clove, grated with a zester

1 Fresno chile or red jalapeño, seeded and finely chopped

2 jarred Calabrian chiles, seeded and finely chopped

2 Tbsp finely chopped shallot

Grated zest of 1 lemon

1 tsp grated orange zest

1 cup [240 ml] olive oil

1 tsp sherry or red wine vinegar

½ tsp salt

½ tsp red pepper flakes

Finely chop the cilantro, parsley, and oregano and put in a large bowl. Add the garlic, Fresno chile, Calabrian chiles, shallot, lemon zest, orange zest, olive oil, vinegar, salt, and pepper flakes and mix thoroughly. Store in a covered container in the refrigerator for up to 3 days.

Mexican sriracha

Mexican sriracha is one of the hot sauces served at Bar Amá. It combines the heat of arbol chiles and the tart-sweet savoriness of tomatoes with the umami of fish sauce. On a spiciness level, arbol chiles are right between chipotle (on the lower end) and pequin (higher). I love their crimson color and bright sharpness. Like Thai sriracha, this sauce includes vinegar and a hit of garlic, but also a lot of fresh aromatic shallots.

MAKES ABOUT 1½ CUPS [355 ML]

1½ Tbsp olive oil

1½ cups [45 g] dried arbol chiles

½ cup [120 ml] tomato sauce or canned crushed tomatoes

1 cup [160 g] sliced shallots

3 Tbsp sugar

7 garlic cloves, peeled

½ cup [120 ml] fish sauce, or to taste, preferably Three Crabs or Red Boat

Scant ½ cup [100 ml] distilled white vinegar

½ cup [120 ml] water, or as needed

Heat the olive oil in a large frying pan over medium-high heat until hot and shimmering. Add the chiles, tomato sauce, shallots, sugar, and garlic. Turn the heat to high and cook, stirring often, until the chiles and shallots soften, about 6 minutes. Remove from the heat and set aside to cool.

Once cool, put the chile mixture, fish sauce (there's no salt in this recipe because fish sauce is fairly salty), and vinegar in the blender and blend on high speed, adding water a tablespoon at a time, until liquefied, about 5 minutes. Use just enough water to blend the mixture to the consistency of a smooth sauce. Taste and add more fish sauce as desired.

Strain the mixture through a chinois or fine-mesh strainer and into a lidded jar. Discard the solids. Store in the refrigerator for up to 2 weeks.

Ghee

Golden, rich ghee is what I use to make the flatbread (page 176) at Bäco Mercat. You can also use it to cook just about anything, just as you would oil (ghee doesn't contain milk solids, so it has a higher smoke point than butter). To make ghee, you heat butter until its three components—butterfat, milk solids, and water—separate. The water will evaporate, the milk solids will sink to the bottom of the pan and caramelize, and the rest is pure butterfat. (The difference between clarified butter and ghee? For clarified butter, you don't want the butter solids to brown at all.) Making ghee is a "two-foam" process: keep an eye on the butter, and you will see it foam up once, settle down, then foam again. This is when the milk solids start to brown, the butterfat turns golden, and you'll smell nutty, toasty deliciousness. Then you have liquid gold.

MAKES ABOUT 1½ CUPS [315 G]

2 cups [455 g] butter

Prepare an ice bath by filling a large bowl with ice water. Set aside.

Cut the butter into several pieces and put them in a saucepan over medium-high heat. Heat the butter, stirring occasionally, until it melts completely, about 5 minutes.

Turn the heat to medium so that the milk solids do not brown too quickly; continue to simmer. As the water separates from the butter and evaporates, it will foam for a few minutes, then subside. The length of time will vary depending on the water content of your butter.

Continue to simmer. After a few minutes (again, the time will vary), the butter will foam again, then become increasingly clear. Watch closely. When the milk solids begin to brown, the butterfat will be golden and clear, and you will smell a slightly nutty fragrance. Remove from the heat immediately, as the solids can quickly burn.

Transfer the saucepan to the ice bath to stop the cooking process and ensure the brown butter solids don't burn. Cool for 1 minute in the ice bath, then remove the saucepan and set aside for several minutes so that the milk solids continue to settle. Carefully pour the clear butterfat—this is the ghee—through a fine-mesh or cheesecloth-lined strainer into a heat-resistant bowl, leaving the solids in the pan. Set aside.

What's left in the pan are browned milk solids, and these are worth saving. Scrape the browned solids from the pan, using a metal spoon, and place in a covered container. This can be stored in the refrigerator for up to 1 month and used for adding to sauces, pastas, custards, or baked goods for its rich nuttiness.

Store the ghee in a covered container in the refrigerator for up to 1 month.

Aonori mascarpone butter

Fresh butter is easy to make using an electric mixer, and the lush, velvety, sweet results are extremely delicious. Straight from the mixer and just strained from its buttermilk, the butter gets folded with mascarpone, aonori (ground dried Japanese seaweed), and a little bit of sea salt. The combination of sweet fresh butter and dried seaweed is a winning one, and the mascarpone makes it extra rich and extra light at the same time. Smear it on crusty bread, swirl it into pasta—it's actually hard not to eat it by the spoonful.

NOTE: Aonori is available at Japanese markets and online.

MAKES ABOUT 1¾ CUPS [365 G]

3 cups [710 ml] heavy cream
⅔ cup [140 g] mascarpone
½ tsp aonori
¼ tsp flaky sea salt, or to taste

Pour the cream into a stand mixer fitted with the whisk attachment and cover the bowl with plastic wrap so that you won't be splashed with buttermilk. Beat the cream on medium speed. After several minutes, it will form soft peaks, followed by stiff peaks. The cream will start to look yellow, and the yellow clumps of butter will suddenly separate from the liquid buttermilk. As soon as it does, turn off the mixer. This takes about 10 minutes.

Set a fine-mesh strainer over a bowl. Pour the contents of the mixer into the strainer so that the buttermilk drains into the bowl. Knead the butter with your hands in the strainer until it is smooth and dense, 2 to 3 minutes. The remaining buttermilk can be strained again through a fine-mesh strainer or cheesecloth and stored in a covered container in the refrigerator for up to 1 week.

Transfer the butter to a medium bowl and fold in the mascarpone, aonori, and salt. Store in a covered container in the refrigerator for up to 2 weeks.

Yogurt in a jar

You don't need a yogurt machine to make fresh yogurt at home—just a thermometer and a jar. The best milk you can source results in the best possible yogurt. You'll notice that different types of milk will affect the flavor of the yogurt. I like that cream-top milk gives you cream-top yogurt, fresh and custardy.

MAKES ABOUT 4 CUPS [1 KG]

4 cups [950 ml] best-quality whole milk
⅓ cup [90 g] yogurt with live, active cultures

Bring a large pot of water to a boil.

Meanwhile, prepare a 1-qt [1-L] glass jar or two 1-pt [500-ml] jars by washing the jars and lids thoroughly. Carefully pour the boiling water into the jars to sterilize them, let stand for several minutes, then carefully pour out the water. Set the jars aside.

Heat the milk in a saucepan until it reaches 180° to 185°F [80° to 85°C] on a candy or instant-read thermometer. Remove from the heat.

Cool the milk to 110° to 115°F [45° to 50°C]. Add the yogurt to the milk, stir, and pour the now inoculated mixture into the jars. Seal the lids and let stand in a warm place, such as an oven that hasn't been turned on, for 7 to 10 hours. The longer it sits out, the more pronounced its tang will be.

Refrigerate the yogurt for at least 1 hour before serving; it will thicken as it cools. Store in lidded jars in the refrigerator for up to 10 days.

Fresh ricotta

Fresh, curdy ricotta is fast and easy to make and requires just a few ingredients. Delicate, milky, sweet, and slightly tangy, it is best eaten immediately, served warm in a bowl with flaky sea salt, coarsely ground black pepper, and a drizzle of good olive oil, or serve it for dessert with fresh berries and honey.

MAKES ABOUT 2 CUPS [500 G]

4 cups [950 ml] best-quality whole milk
½ cup [120 ml] heavy cream
¼ cup [70 g] plain yogurt
1½ tsp fresh lemon juice
½ tsp salt

In a medium saucepan, whisk together the milk, cream, yogurt, lemon juice, and salt until smooth. Bring the mixture to a boil over medium-high heat, stirring occasionally. Turn the heat to medium-low and simmer until the mixture curdles, stirring constantly, about 2 minutes. You'll see the curds (about the size of small cottage cheese curds) separate from the whey.

In a cheesecloth-lined fine-mesh sieve or colander set over a bowl, let the curds drain for 5 minutes. Discard the liquid. Use immediately or store in a covered container in the refrigerator for up to 2 days.

Cacik

Cacik is the traditional Turkish yogurt dip with mint, cucumber, olive oil, garlic, lemon juice, and salt. For complex-flavored heat, I'll add a bit of yuzu kosho, the Japanese fermented citrus and chile paste. You could also use harrough (page 42) or even a little bit of pounded raw chile such as habanero. Add just a tiny amount at a time and check the heat level; it can get spicy fast. The yuzu kosho is salty, so taste and adjust accordingly. I also like adding raisins for their chewy sweetness and walnuts for their crunch. This is also a base for buttermilk-cacik soup (page 214).

NOTE: High-quality bottled yuzu kosho is available at Japanese markets and online.

MAKES 1¾ CUPS [490 G]

¼ cup [30 g] walnuts

1½ cups [405 g] Greek yogurt

1 cucumber, preferably Persian, grated and squeezed with a towel

Heaping 1 Tbsp golden raisins

1 tsp grated lemon zest

1 tsp yuzu kosho

½ garlic clove, grated with a zester

½ Tbsp fresh lemon juice

2 Tbsp extra-virgin olive oil

Salt

½ Tbsp honey (optional)

20 fresh mint leaves

Heat the oven to 350°F [180°C]. Spread the walnuts in a single layer in a baking dish and place on a middle rack in the oven. Roast, stirring the nuts once for even cooking, until toasty and fragrant, 12 to 15 minutes. Set aside to cool.

Put the yogurt in a large bowl. Coarsely chop the grated cucumber. Add the cucumber, toasted nuts, raisins, lemon zest, yuzu kosho, garlic, lemon juice, and olive oil to the bowl. Season with salt and honey (if using). Tear the mint leaves over the yogurt mixture in the bowl. Whisk gently until combined. Use immediately or store in a covered container in the refrigerator for up to 2 days.

Crème fraîche

MAKES ABOUT 2 CUPS [480 G]

2 Tbsp buttermilk
2 cups [480 ml] heavy cream

Bring a kettle of water to a boil.

Meanwhile, prepare a 1-pt [500-ml] glass jar by washing the jar and lid thoroughly. Carefully pour the boiling water into the jar to sterilize, let stand for several minutes, then carefully pour out the water.

Combine the buttermilk and heavy cream in the jar. Seal the lid and let stand at room temperature (about 70°F [21°C]) until very thick, 8 to 24 hours. Store in the refrigerator for up to 10 days.

Creamy dill dressing

Like spices, fresh herbs are key to flavor and maybe even more versatile—they can be used as either a main component in a dish or a highlighting garnish. In this dressing, dill is everything. This recipe calls for a lot of it. I love the herb's sweet, citrusy, and anise-like flavor in sauces (such as tomato sauce for pasta), soups, dressings, and tonics, as much as in salads.

MAKES ABOUT 1 CUP [240 ML]

1 cup [240 g] crème fraîche (facing page)

½ cup [7 g] dill fronds, finely chopped

1 garlic clove, grated with a zester

1 tsp finely chopped shallot

1 tsp chopped fresh chives

1 tsp grated lemon zest

Juice of 1 lemon

½ tsp salt

Fresh black pepper

Mix the crème fraîche, dill, garlic, shallot, chives, lemon zest, lemon juice, salt, and a few grinds of black pepper in a medium bowl. Serve immediately or store covered in the refrigerator for up to 2 days.

I love juicy, crunchy vegetables like endive, snap peas, fennel, and cucumbers, along with lots of fresh green herbs—the snappy stuff of salads. I mean *salad* in a broad sense, from elegant, simple, and leafy to a lot of textures, colors, and flavors. The sensibility is less spa food than *zakuski*, the Russian party buffet of overflowing snacks and appetizers. Exuberant. That's how vegetables make me feel.

Salads especially are about both juxtaposition and balance. Ingredients are layered, but each should also be distinct. There should be a range of sensory-stimulating elements: the crunch of fresh vegetables, the aroma of herbs and spices, the appeal of shapes and colors. This also gives a cook a lot of latitude; there could be any number of combinations for a salad already in the refrigerator.

In Southern California, we have access to some of the best and most varied locally grown produce throughout the year. I'm always waiting for what the next week will bring: wildflower blossoms, morels, nettles, fingerling potatoes, sunchokes, scarlet onions, baby radishes the size of the tip of my pinkie, Ogen melons almost half the size of my head.

Because they're so varied—in flavor, color, and texture—vegetables are easy to experiment with, easier than meats for sure. They take to bright, tangy vinaigrettes, creamy dressings, and heady, complex spices. The experience of eating them changes with the way they are cut or torn, whether they are cooked or raw.

Spring and summer are inspiring because of the sheer amount of vegetables that are available. When it's warm by February (which often happens in L.A.), even the first of the strawberries at farmers' markets can be ripe and sweet and juicy. They signal the coming parade of spring's green vegetables: the artichokes, English peas, fava beans, snap peas, and asparagus, which get fatter and fatter as the season progresses.

There are so many vegetables that I almost forget about lettuces entirely. Lettuces have to be snappy and succulent, too. I like sturdy romaines like Little Gems, or Batavian crispheads that have both crunchy cores and layers of soft leaves. My favorite leafy salad vegetable is Castelfranco, which is a lettuce-like radicchio (or chicory) that's pleasantly bitter and speckled. Leaves other than lettuces and chicories that are also great for salads: arugula, mizuna, mustard greens, and pea tips (which include the leaves, stems, blossoms, and tendrils).

I use whatever's at hand. Maybe it's early spring and the asparagus is really getting going and cool-weather fennel is still in the markets. This is also when young green almonds, which have soft, gelatinous seeds, are around. So I make a salad by shaving asparagus, fennel, and ricotta salata, then toss with green almonds and dress with a light dukkah vinaigrette. Or I grill the asparagus and mix it with blanched English peas, harissa vinaigrette, and lemon crème fraîche. More vegetables appear . . . and so I serve crudités with a dozen kinds of vegetables, fruit, and herbs.

Even the most delicate of vegetables take to a full spectrum of seasonings and flavors, bolder than you might think.

fresh

green

snappy

light

Castelfranco with cheddar and miso-fenugreek dressing

My favorite vegetable for leafy salad isn't a lettuce. It's Castelfranco, a mild radicchio with ruffled pale green or yellow leaves that are burgundy-speckled. The tender leaves grow in a rose-like cluster and are both slightly sweet and slightly bitter. They're delicate but stand up to other big flavors, like aged cheddar and bitter herbs. The dressing for this salad isn't sleepy, either. There are a lot of ingredients that result in crazy (in a good way) flavor: white miso, soy sauce, citrus, and rice vinegar mixed with the herb fenugreek and spices urfa biber and sumac, along with grated fresh ginger. It hits all the umami, tart, bright, and spicy notes.

NOTE: Standard radicchio can be substituted for Castelfranco radicchio. You can substitute the urfa biber with Aleppo pepper or any coarsely ground, dried, mildly spicy chile, such as New Mexico chile or cascabel, or red pepper flakes. High-quality bottled yuzu juice is available at Japanese markets and online.

SERVES 4

1 tsp white sesame seeds

2 heads Castelfranco radicchio, ends trimmed and outer leaves removed

¼ cup [35 g] salted roasted Marcona almonds

4 oz [115 g] aged white cheddar, crumbled

½ bunch parsley, leaves only

¼ cup [60 ml] extra-virgin olive oil

2 Tbsp white miso

2 Tbsp yuzu juice or fresh lemon juice

1 Tbsp soy sauce

1 Tbsp rice vinegar

1 tsp toasted sesame oil

1 tsp urfa biber

½ tsp grated peeled fresh ginger

½ tsp ground sumac

½ tsp dried or fresh fenugreek leaves

Toast the sesame seeds in a small, dry frying pan over medium heat, stirring frequently, until golden brown and fragrant, 1 to 2 minutes. Remove from the heat and set aside.

Tear the Castelfranco leaves into large pieces and put them in a large bowl along with the almonds, cheddar, and parsley. Set aside.

Whisk together the olive oil, miso, yuzu juice, soy sauce, rice vinegar, and sesame oil in another bowl. Add the toasted sesame seeds, urfa biber, ginger, sumac, and fenugreek and whisk to combine. This makes about ¾ cup [180 ml] dressing. Toss the Castelfranco mixture with the dressing to taste. Serve immediately.

Cabbage slaw with crème fraîche, mitsuba, and kochkocha

This cabbage slaw brings together spicy-bright kochkocha (Ethiopian hot sauce) and tangy crème fraîche. Add a couple of big handfuls of mitsuba, the wild Japanese parsley that's kind of a cross between flat-leaf parsley and shiso. It also reminds me of both chervil and celery leaf, clean and refreshing. Mitsuba is slightly bitter, the cabbage a little sweet and crunchy, and the kochkocha spicy with chiles and slightly floral from the cardamom.

NOTE: You can substitute the kochkocha with a pinch of freshly toasted and ground cardamom, a pinch of freshly toasted and ground cumin, and ½ serrano or 1 Thai chile, finely chopped. Mitsuba is available at Japanese markets and farmers' markets.

SERVES 4

½ head green cabbage, cored and outer leaves removed

1 lemon, halved

Salt

½ cup [120 g] crème fraîche (page 94)

1 tsp kochkocha (page 82)

Fresh black pepper

½ tsp sherry vinegar

Pinch of piment d'Espelette

2 small bunches mitsuba, leaves only

Cut the cabbage into ½-in [12-mm] slices and put them in a large bowl. Squeeze the juice of ½ lemon over the cabbage and toss with a pinch of salt. Set aside.

Whisk together the crème fraîche, kochkocha, a pinch of salt, 4 grinds of black pepper, the juice of the remaining ½ lemon, the sherry vinegar, and the piment d'Espelette in a medium bowl. Pour the mixture over the cabbage, add the mitsuba, and gently but thoroughly mix, using a wooden spoon. Serve immediately.

Red endive and blood oranges with blue cheese, dukkah, and Banyuls vinaigrette

Bitter-leafed chicories—radicchio, puntarelle, Belgian endive, and less bitter escarole—are one of my favorite salad ingredients. I especially like Belgian red endive, which is technically forced radicchio, grown so that the leaf-stem clusters remain tightly bunched but are still burgundy along the edges. These leaves are refreshingly bitter, sweet, and nutty, delicate and smooth on the surface but sturdy and crunchy, too. That's what makes them ideal for composed salads and a good pairing with richer ingredients: nuts, cheese, caviar, smoked fish, crème fraîche, duck confit, chicken liver, bacon. Belgian red endive is just as complementary to sweet and tart fruit: apples and pears, citrus, berries, dates, and persimmons. This simple salad mixes red endive and blood oranges (love these colors) with one of my go-to cheeses, blue cheese; I always have it around. Garnish with a little piment d'Espelette or Aleppo pepper and a handful of dukkah.

NOTE: Look for a young blue cheese with a fudgy but slightly dry texture, such as Point Reyes Bay Blue or Stilton. Sherry vinegar can be substituted for Banyuls vinegar.

SERVES 4

4 or 5 blood oranges

3 Belgian red endives, trimmed and leaves separated

1 Tbsp chopped fresh tarragon

1 Tbsp chopped dill fronds

1 Tbsp chopped fresh parsley

cont'd

⅓ cup [25 g] caraway croutons (page 54, optional)

4 oz [115 g] blue cheese, crumbled

1 Tbsp Banyuls vinegar

Pinch of salt

3 Tbsp extra-virgin olive oil

1 tsp finely chopped shallot

1 tsp chopped fresh chives

1 tsp grated lemon zest

Fresh black pepper

3 Tbsp Virginia peanut and coriander dukkah (page 47)
or hazelnut and fennel dukkah (page 48)

¼ tsp piment d'Espelette or Aleppo pepper

TO PREPARE THE BLOOD ORANGES: Trim a little off the top and bottom of
each orange with a sharp knife so that there are two flat ends. Set an
orange flat on a cutting surface and cut away the peel and white skin
from top to bottom, working your way around the fruit. Repeat with
each blood orange. Cut each blood orange crosswise into ½-in [12-mm]
slices. Set aside.

Toss together the endive, tarragon, dill, parsley, and croutons (if using)
in a large bowl. Gently mix in the blue cheese. Set aside.

Whisk together the Banyuls vinegar and salt in a medium bowl.
Add the olive oil, shallot, chives, lemon zest, and several grinds of
black pepper. Gently toss the endive mixture with the dressing.

Sprinkle with the dukkah and piment d'Espelette.
Transfer to a platter and serve immediately.

Snap pea and Asian pear salad with grapefruit, burrata, and hazelnuts

The inspiration for this salad started out as a take on the Levantine bread salad fattoush. I originally used snap peas and Asian pear instead of the traditional cucumbers and tomatoes, and burrata instead of feta. It has since evolved, mainly with the addition of grapefruit. And then I also replaced fried torn pieces of flatbread with crunchy nuts (sometimes walnuts, sometimes hazelnuts). There are a lot of textures and flavors—the snappy peas, crisp and juicy Asian pear, creamy burrata, fleshy grapefruit, and crunchy hazelnuts—so it's dressed simply with a garlic-laced walnut vinaigrette and, in a nod to fattoush, sprinkled with sumac.

SERVES 4

WALNUT VINAIGRETTE

⅓ cup [80 ml] sherry vinegar

1½ tsp salt

Fresh black pepper

½ cup [120 ml] walnut oil

2 Tbsp olive oil

2 tsp grated shallot

1 garlic clove, peeled

1 cup [155 g] sugar snap peas, trimmed

2 grapefruits

1 Belgian endive, trimmed and leaves separated

2 Asian pears, cored and cut into thin slices

4 French breakfast radishes, quartered lengthwise

2 Tbsp chopped fresh tarragon

2 Tbsp chopped dill fronds

2 Tbsp chopped fresh parsley

2 Tbsp chopped fresh chervil

8 oz [230 g] burrata

⅓ cup [55 g] coarsely chopped hazelnuts

Ground sumac for garnish (optional)

cont'd

MAKE THE VINAIGRETTE: Whisk together the sherry vinegar and salt in a small bowl. Add 3 or 4 grinds of black pepper and the walnut oil, olive oil, and shallot. Grate the garlic into the bowl with a zester and whisk again to combine. Set aside. (This makes more vinaigrette than is called for here. Store the remaining dressing in a covered container, refrigerated, for up to 1 week.)

Prepare an ice bath by filling a large bowl with ice water. Set aside. Bring a medium pot of salted water to a boil over high heat. Add the snap peas and blanch until just tender, about 1 minute. Use a strainer or skimmer to transfer them to the ice bath to cool. Drain and set aside.

TO SEGMENT THE GRAPEFRUITS: Trim a little off the top and bottom of each grapefruit with a sharp knife so that there are two flat ends. Set a grapefruit flat on a cutting surface and cut away the peel and white skin from top to bottom, working your way around the fruit. Remove each citrus segment by cutting between the fruit and the membrane; the wedges should release easily. Transfer to a small bowl and set aside.

Toss together the snap peas, endive, Asian pears, radishes, tarragon, dill, parsley, and chervil in a large bowl. Whisk the walnut vinaigrette again and add ⅓ cup [80 ml] to the salad and gently toss. Add the grapefruit segments and gently toss again.

Divide the burrata, spooning a piece onto each of four plates. Place the snap pea mixture on top of the burrata, dividing it evenly. Sprinkle each plate with the hazelnuts and sumac, if desired. Drizzle with more of the dressing, if desired. Serve immediately.

Tuscan melon and Persian cucumber salad with cacik

Peak-season melons come during the height of summer in Los Angeles, when farmers' market stands are piled high with all kinds: Charentais, Galia, Ogen, cantaloupe, white honeydew. One of my favorites is Tuscan melon, which has a netted rind with green or golden grooves, a musky perfume, and rich, creamy, orange flesh that's especially sweet. Their fruity sweetness makes them a good match with vibrant herbs like dill and basil. I also like the combination of creamy melon with crunchy Persian (or English) cucumbers and earthy walnuts.

SERVES 4

⅓ cup [40 g] whole walnuts

6 cucumbers, preferably Persian, about 1⅓ lb [600 g] total

1 Tuscan melon or cantaloupe, about 2 lb [910 g], cut into thin slices

2 Tbsp torn dill fronds

10 fresh basil leaves

½ tsp salt

2 tsp fresh lemon juice

1 Tbsp olive oil

½ cup [140 g] cacik (page 92)

½ tsp piment d'Espelette or Aleppo pepper

Heat the oven to 350°F [180°C]. Spread the walnuts in a single layer in a baking dish and place on a middle rack in the oven. Roast, stirring the nuts once for even cooking, until toasty and fragrant, 12 to 15 minutes. Set aside to cool.

Trim the cucumbers and cut them in half lengthwise, then cut them into thick slices on the bias. Put the melon and cucumber in a medium bowl. Add the dill, basil, salt, walnuts, lemon juice, and olive oil and toss until combined.

Place 2 Tbsp cacik on the bottom of each of four plates or shallow bowls. Divide the melon and cucumber salad evenly on top of the cacik. Sprinkle each with a pinch of piment d'Espelette. Serve immediately.

Salted cucumbers with avocado and ginger-soy dressing

The salted cucumbers and radicchio are a sharp, slightly pickled contrast to creamy, sweet avocado. I like the spicy punch of a little Aleppo pepper and urfa biber in the spice mixture shichimi togarashi with the Japanese flavors of soy sauce, ginger, sesame oil, and mirin. The Japanese fermented chile-and-citrus paste yuzu kosho is key, with its spicy, funky, citrusy, salty flavors.

NOTE: High-quality bottled yuzu kosho is available at Japanese markets and online. You can substitute toasted sesame seeds for the urfa biber shichimi togarashi.

SERVES 4

6 cucumbers, preferably Persian or Japanese, about 1⅓ lb [600 g] total
1 head radicchio
½ Tbsp kosher salt
½ cup [120 ml] rice vinegar
2 Tbsp soy sauce
2 Tbsp sesame oil
2 Tbsp mirin
1 tsp yuzu kosho
1 tsp grated peeled fresh ginger
2 avocados, peeled, pitted, and cut into thin slices
Pinch of flaky sea salt
1 scallion, green part only, cut into thin slices on the bias
1 Tbsp urfa biber shichimi togarashi (page 38)

Trim the cucumbers and cut them in half lengthwise, then cut them into thick slices on the bias. Put them in a large bowl and set aside.

Cut the radicchio into quarters. Tear the outer leaves into bite-size pieces, discarding the base and heart. Put the radicchio into the bowl with the cucumbers, toss with the kosher salt, and let stand for 10 minutes. Lightly rinse the radicchio and cucumbers in a colander; gently squeeze and dry on paper towels.

In a large bowl, toss the cucumbers with the radicchio. Whisk together the rice vinegar, soy sauce, sesame oil, mirin, yuzu kosho, and ginger in a small bowl and toss with the cucumber and radicchio. Gently stir in the avocado. Sprinkle with the flaky sea salt, scallion, and shichimi togarashi. Serve immediately.

Fennel, kale, shaved cauliflower, and apple with creamy dill dressing and bacon bread crumb persillade

Fall and wintertime produce make for some outstanding cool-weather salads. In peak season, through the fall and into early spring, anise-flavored fennel, bitter kale, and mild cauliflower are a really good match with sweet-crisp apple. In this case, the kale, cauliflower, fennel, and apple are all thinly sliced and raw—for a hit of snappy freshness in the middle of winter. Finish with black pepper, citrusy dill, and salty ricotta salata. Persillade is parsley (or *persil* in French) chopped together with garlic, herbs, oil, or vinegar—made better with bacon.

SERVES 4

3 to 5 Tuscan kale leaves, center ribs removed

1 Honeycrisp apple

4 oz [115 g] cauliflower florets

½ fennel bulb

2 tsp finely chopped shallot

2 tsp chopped fresh chives

2 tsp grated lemon zest

¼ tsp salt

Fresh black pepper

1 Tbsp chopped dill fronds

2 Tbsp creamy dill dressing (page 95)

½ oz [15 g] ricotta salata

2 Tbsp bacon bread crumb persillade (page 55)

Cut the kale leaves into 1-in [2.5-cm] strips and put them in a large bowl. Quarter, core, and cut the apple into ¼-in [6-mm] slices and add them to the bowl. Cut the cauliflower and fennel into very thin slices with a mandoline and add them to the bowl.

Toss the kale mixture with the shallot, chives, lemon zest, salt, a few grinds of black pepper, the dill, and the creamy dill dressing. Transfer to a platter. Shave the ricotta salata over the top of the salad using a mandoline or vegetable peeler. Sprinkle the bacon bread crumb persillade over the top. Serve immediately.

Crudités with walnut-miso bagna cauda

You eat a crudités platter like this when you feel like celebrating. It features the best fruits and vegetables possible, some served raw and others roasted, so that you get different textures and temperatures. It's easy to riff on these by using what's in season. I like a fall-winter mix of Asian pears, Brussels sprouts, broccolini, radishes, and certain varieties of avocado. In the spring, I incorporate asparagus, carrots, artichoke hearts, English peas, grapefruit, or even strawberries. In the summer, it's stone fruit and mulberries, cucumbers, haricots verts, maybe pickled okra. For dipping: herbal vinaigrettes, spicy sauces, or bright creamy dressings. Bagna cauda is the warm Piedmontese dip typically made with garlic, anchovies, olive oil, and butter. The version served here is enriched with miso, walnuts, and sesame paste.

NOTE: You can substitute the walnut-miso bagna cauda with creamy dill dressing (page 95), or serve both.

SERVES 4 TO 6

15 Brussels sprouts, halved

½ large head cauliflower, broken into bite-size florets

1 bunch broccolini, trimmed

2 Tbsp olive oil, plus more for garnish

½ tsp kosher salt

8 small carrots, peeled and halved lengthwise

1 small ripe avocado, peeled, pitted, and cut into thin wedges

6 French breakfast or watermelon radishes, halved or quartered lengthwise, depending on size

½ Asian pear, cored and cut into thin wedges

1 tsp finely chopped fresh parsley

2 tsp finely chopped fresh chives

½ lemon

Flaky sea salt

Fresh black pepper

½ cup [85 g] walnut-miso bagna cauda (page 56), warmed

Heat the oven to 500°F [260°C]. Put the Brussels sprouts, cauliflower, and broccolini on a baking sheet, add the 2 Tbsp olive oil, and toss to coat. Sprinkle with the kosher salt. Roast until tender but still snappy and browned in spots, about 15 minutes.

To serve, arrange the roasted vegetables, carrots, avocado, radishes, and Asian pear on a platter and sprinkle with the parsley and chives. Drizzle with more oil and squeeze the juice from the lemon over the top. Season with flaky sea salt to taste and a few grinds of black pepper. Serve immediately with the bagna cauda on the side.

Blistered green beans with fenugreek-chipotle tomato sauce

This is my favorite way to serve green beans, blistered at the edges, roasted just to al dente, tossed with a tomato sauce that's perfumed with fenugreek leaves and smoky with chipotle chiles, and topped with fresh herbs. It's also my favorite way to prepare okra.

SERVES 4

2 Tbsp olive oil

12 oz [340 g] green beans, trimmed, or okra, halved lengthwise

½ tsp salt

1 tsp chopped garlic

1 Tbsp sherry vinegar

¼ lime

1 cup [325 g] fenugreek-chipotle tomato sauce (page 67), warmed

20 fresh cilantro leaves, torn

10 fresh basil leaves, torn

10 fresh mint leaves, torn

1 tsp arbol-guajillo furikake (page 39, optional)

Heat the oven to 375°F [190°C].

Heat the olive oil in a large cast-iron frying pan over medium-high heat until hot and shimmering. Add the green beans and ¼ tsp of the salt and turn the heat to high. Sauté, stirring occasionally, until the green beans begin to char at the edges, about 2 minutes.

Transfer the pan to the oven, sprinkle with garlic, and roast the green beans until cooked but still al dente, 3 to 5 minutes. Remove from the oven and add the sherry vinegar and the remaining ¼ tsp salt. Squeeze the juice from the lime over the green beans. Add the tomato sauce and toss to coat.

Transfer the green beans to a large serving platter and garnish with the torn cilantro, basil, and mint, along with furikake, if desired. Serve immediately.

It's no coincidence that almost all of the vegetables in this chapter are brassicas: a genus of flowering plants collectively known as the mustards, the crucifers, or the cabbage family. Surprisingly, cauliflower is one of the best-selling dishes at the restaurants, especially a dish of chartreuse-colored Romanesco (the most beautiful vegetable I know) roasted with radicchio and pea tendrils and seasoned with yuzu, dashi, and piment d'Espelette.

In an era of hardy-greens worship, I barely remember a time when I didn't cook a lot of cauliflower, Brussels sprouts, broccolini, and kale. But the only kale that I knew growing up was the decorative purple variety that grew around the perimeter of my high school. Nobody ever thought to eat them, or much of any other kind of kale.

Now it seems like everyone's favorite vegetable, part of a fairly big family that includes Brussels sprouts, cabbages, kohlrabi, broccoli, and cauliflower. They come from the same plant, a wild Mediterranean cabbage, and what makes each distinct is the result of thousands of years of human cultivation and selective propagating. Radishes, spicy cresses, mustards, several Asian greens, rutabagas, and turnips belong to other brassica species.

These are some of my favorite sturdy vegetables because of their bold shapes and great textures: leathery kale, crunchy Romanesco and kohlrabi, the flower heads of broccoli, curdy cauliflower, rosettes of cabbages. I like the buds, roots, stems, leaves, and flowers of so many of these vegetables, but compared with other brassicas (like mustards), they're pretty mild in flavor.

Unless you're using them raw or blanched for salads, I think the key to getting the most from these is often by caramelization (or, more accurately, the Maillard reaction) for more complex flavor and good color. And by good color, I mean those well-browned edges that come with searing, sautéing, grilling, and/or roasting. Those crisped browned edges mean flavor.

That's the starting point, and from there the question is, how can I make broccoli, cauliflower, and kale taste next-level delicious? Like with so many other dishes, acid is supreme (following salt). I think brassicas and citrus—lemons, Meyer lemons, yuzu—are an especially elegant combination.

I try not to rely too heavily on aromatics such as garlic and onions. They don't open up and brighten flavor like lemons. And though I love vinegar, including strong red vinegar and sherry vinegar, the citric acid of lemon juice is fresh and clean and relatively delicate. Tart, floral, vibrant citrus are a good match for brassicas that are earthy, nutty, slightly bitter, and a little sweet.

bright

citrusy

zesty

hardy

Creamy Romanesco soup with grapefruit, nigella, and fresh horseradish

Romanesco is almost too stunning a vegetable to purée, but I don't let that stop me, because it makes for a delicious creamy soup (in a pretty shade of green). I might swirl in pistou; garnish it with finely chopped celery, celery leaves, shallots, and some grated lemon zest; or add a little pancetta and caramelized onion. Here, citrus and horseradish balance the richness of the soup.

SERVES 4

1 grapefruit

1 large head Romanesco, about 1 lb [455 g], trimmed

2 cups [480 ml] vegetable broth or water

2 cups [480 ml] heavy cream

Salt

1 Tbsp sugar

½ tsp nigella seeds

Fresh horseradish root for garnish

TO SEGMENT THE GRAPEFRUIT: Trim a little off the top and bottom of the grapefruit with a sharp knife so that there are two flat ends. Set the grapefruit flat on a cutting surface and cut away the peel and white skin from top to bottom, working your way around the fruit. Remove each citrus segment by cutting between the fruit and the membrane for each section; the wedges should release easily. Set aside.

Cut the Romanesco into ½-in [12-mm] slices; the florets will fall apart into pieces. Transfer to a large saucepan or stockpot. Add the broth, cream, and a pinch of salt and bring to a boil over high heat. Lower the heat to a simmer and cook until the Romanesco is tender, about 10 minutes. Remove from the heat.

Carefully remove 1 cup [240 ml] of the cooking liquid and set aside. In a blender or with a stick blender, blend the Romanesco and remaining liquid until smooth. Add more of the cooking liquid as needed until velvety. The soup should coat the back of a spoon and have a nappe consistency (if you run your finger along the back of the coated spoon, you should see a clean line). Add the sugar and 1 Tbsp salt and blend. Taste and adjust the seasoning as desired.

Divide the soup among four bowls. Garnish each with a few segments of grapefruit and a sprinkling of nigella. Use a zester to grate a couple of strikes of fresh horseradish over each bowl. Serve immediately.

Roasted Romanesco and Treviso radicchio with yuzu and dashi

Romanesco cauliflower, with its lime green color and spiral-on-spiral florets, is an especially striking vegetable. It tastes like the familiar white cauliflower but slightly nuttier—and earthy and grassy and slightly sweet. It gets a little sweeter with roasting. Here, it's mixed with bitter Treviso radicchio, a very concentrated dashi, and tart yuzu. Dashi and yuzu are one of my favorite combinations: one is deep and resonant with umami, and the other is sour, floral, and bright.

NOTE: You can substitute the dashi concentrate with bottled shiro dashi, available in Japanese markets, often in the same section as soy sauce and tsuyu (dipping sauce for noodles). Try to avoid the brands that contain MSG because they tend to be saltier. It usually is sold as a concentrate, and I recommend diluting it 3 parts shiro dashi to 2 parts water. High-quality bottled yuzu juice is available at Japanese markets and online.

SERVES 4

1 tsp white sesame seeds

2 Tbsp avocado or olive oil

1 medium head Romanesco, about 12 oz [340 g], trimmed and cut into bite-size florets

¼ tsp salt

1 garlic clove, finely chopped

3 tsp finely chopped shallot

1 cup [20 g] pea tips (including leaves, stems, and tendrils)

2½ Tbsp dashi concentrate (page 76)

2½ Tbsp yuzu juice

½ head Treviso radicchio, about 4 oz [115 g], trimmed and cut into 1½-in [4-cm] pieces

1 Tbsp plus 1 tsp chopped fresh chives

¼ tsp piment d'Espelette

¼ tsp grated lemon zest

Heat the oven to 450°F [230°C].

Toast the sesame seeds in a small, dry frying pan over medium heat, stirring frequently, until golden brown and fragrant, 1 to 2 minutes. Remove from the heat and set aside.

cont'd

Heat 1 Tbsp of the oil in a large cast-iron frying pan over high heat until hot and shimmering. Add the Romanesco and salt, tossing to coat, and sauté, stirring occasionally, just until the edges begin to brown, about 1 minute. Add the garlic, remove from the heat, and transfer the pan to the oven.

Roast the Romanesco until it's cooked through but still crunchy, about 5 minutes. Remove from the oven, add the remaining 1 Tbsp oil, and carefully return the pan to the stove over medium-low heat. Add 2 tsp of the shallots and the pea tips and toss. Immediately add the dashi concentrate, yuzu juice, Treviso, and 1 Tbsp of the chives and sauté just until the Treviso wilts, about 1 minute. Don't cook the Treviso too long or it will brown instead of retaining its bright purple color. Remove from the heat.

Sprinkle the piment d'Espelette, toasted sesame seeds, lemon zest, remaining 1 tsp shallots, and remaining 1 tsp chives over the top. Serve immediately.

"Caesar" Brussels sprouts

I found a delivery of 30 pounds of Brussels sprouts in the walk-in refrigerator one day. What do you do with 30 pounds of Brussels sprouts? You get creative. That's how the "Caesar" Brussels sprouts were born. I also happen to love Caesar salad, because the combination of tangy cheese and briny anchovies is genius. This is a salad of Brussels sprouts' leaves and their sliced cores, quickly sautéed so that they're toasty, then tossed with lemony Caesar dressing and a little extra vinegar and olive oil. This dish has it all: hardy Brussels sprouts, parsley for herbal freshness, pickled red onion for another layer of acidity and crunch, the richness of Pecorino and buttery bread crumbs, and of course anchovies.

NOTE: This recipe makes more dressing than you'll need for the Brussels sprouts. Store any remaining dressing in a lidded jar in the refrigerator for up to 1 week. You can also use salted anchovies here, rinsed then soaked in 3 Tbsp of milk for 10 minutes, and drained.

SERVES 4

CAESAR DRESSING
5 oil-packed anchovy fillets
½ cup [60 g] grated Pecorino cheese
Juice of 2 lemons
1 garlic clove, peeled
1 tsp Dijon mustard
1 Tbsp sherry vinegar
1 tsp freshly ground black pepper
Pinch of salt
1 cup [240 ml] extra-virgin olive oil

1 lb [455 g] Brussels sprouts
1 Tbsp butter
1 Tbsp avocado or olive oil
¼ tsp salt
1 Tbsp sherry vinegar
⅓ cup [5 g] fresh parsley leaves
¼ cup [40 g] mint and rose pickled red onions (page 22, optional)
4 radishes, cut into thin slices
3 Tbsp grated Pecorino cheese
2 Tbsp caraway bread crumbs (page 54)
½ Tbsp chopped fresh chives

cont'd

Put the anchovies, Pecorino cheese, lemon juice, garlic, mustard, sherry vinegar, black pepper, and salt in a blender and purée on medium speed until nearly smooth. With the blender running, drizzle in the olive oil and blend until creamy. Set aside.

Carefully trim and core the Brussels sprouts with a paring knife or the sharp tip of a vegetable peeler. Discard the outermost leaves. Peel the leaves of each sprout, putting them in a large bowl, until you reach the paler center. Then cut the centers into thin slices and put them in the same bowl.

Heat the butter and oil over medium-high heat in a large sauté pan. When the butter begins to foam, turn the heat to high, add the Brussels sprouts and salt, and cook, stirring occasionally, until the leaves have wilted and their edges begin to char, about 3 minutes.

Transfer the Brussels sprouts back to the bowl and toss with 3 Tbsp of the Caesar dressing and the sherry vinegar. Gently stir in the parsley, pickled onions, radishes, Pecorino cheese, bread crumbs, and chives. Transfer to a platter and serve immediately.

Kohlrabi with crème fraîche, mint, lemon, and yuzu kosho

Kohlrabi: It looks so weird and tastes so delicious. The cabbage cultivar looks like a root vegetable but its edible bulb and stalks grow above ground. It's especially sweet and mild and slightly spicy—like the heart of a cabbage. When young it can be crisp and juicy like an apple. Because it is usually firmer, I blanch kohlrabi and shock it in an ice bath for a crisp but yielding texture. Wedges of crunchy kohlrabi with rich crème fraîche, lots of lemon zest and juice, mint, and parsley are a surprising salad. Yuzu kosho gives it a little spicy-citrusy heat, and I especially like it with just a little smoky, fruity piment d'Espelette.

NOTE: High-quality bottled yuzu kosho is available at Japanese markets and online.

SERVES 4

2 lb [910 g] kohlrabi, cut into 1-in [2.5-cm] wedges
¼ cup [60 g] crème fraîche (page 94)
Grated zest and juice of 1 lemon
¼ tsp yuzu kosho
Fresh black pepper
Pinch of piment d'Espelette
½ cup [8 g] fresh mint leaves
½ cup [7 g] fresh parsley leaves

Prepare an ice bath by filling a large bowl with ice water. Set aside.

Bring a large pot of salted water to a boil over high heat. Add the kohlrabi and blanch for 1½ minutes; the kohlrabi will be a brighter green and still have crunch. Use a strainer or skimmer to transfer the kohlrabi to the ice bath to cool. Drain.

Put the kohlrabi in a large bowl. Add the crème fraîche, lemon zest, lemon juice, yuzu kosho, a few grinds of black pepper, piment d'Espelette, mint, and parsley. Stir gently with a wooden spoon to combine.

Transfer to a platter and serve immediately.

Flowering choy with lime and fish sauce vinaigrette

Blossoming choy has thin, succulent stems, tender leaves, and slightly spicy florets. These are choy plants in their flowering stage. Plants that have bolted like this, or gone to flower, can be tough and bitter. But sometimes, as in the case of yu choy and bok choy, they make for an unexpectedly delicious crop. These show up at farmers' markets in Los Angeles in early spring. Because the florets have a mustardy kick, blossoming choy is especially delicious doused with a tangy-bright-funky umami-packed lime and fish sauce vinaigrette. Rapini, even better with its blossoms, is a good substitute for flowering choy. The brightness of lime and the fermented fish sauce are good with other brassicas, too: cabbage, Brussels sprouts, and cauliflower.

NOTE: Make the lime and fish sauce vinaigrette the night before or several hours in advance so that the flavors in the dressing have time to meld.

SERVES 4

3 Tbsp avocado or olive oil

6 garlic cloves, cut into thin slices

2 bunches yu choy, gai lan, or rapini, about 8 oz [230 g] total, preferably with flowers

½ cup [120 ml] water

¼ tsp salt

¼ cup [60 ml] lime and fish sauce vinaigrette (page 71)

Juice of ¼ lemon or lime

Heat the oil in a frying pan over medium heat until hot and shimmering. Add the garlic and sauté until it begins to color, about 1 minute. Add the choy, turn the heat to medium-high, and sauté for 1 minute longer. Add the water and continue to cook until the water has evaporated, 1 to 2 minutes. Remove from the heat.

Transfer to a serving dish and toss with the salt and vinaigrette. Squeeze the juice from the lemon over the top. Serve immediately.

Caramelized cauliflower with mint, pine nuts, lime, and yogurt

The nutty, sweet flavor of cauliflower is more pronounced when it's roasted. These cauliflower florets are seared on the stove for crisp-caramelized edges, which give them another layer of flavor, then roasted in the oven so that they're tender and juicy. Bring them back to the stove for just a minute to cook the garlic, shallot, chives, and lemon zest so that they don't burn. I like vegetables with the combination of acid, fresh herbs, and spice. Here, it's lemon, basil, cilantro, mint, and red pepper flakes. A little bit of creamy, honeyed yogurt adds enough richness.

NOTE: You can substitute arbol-guajillo furikake (page 39) for the red pepper flakes.

SERVES 4

2 Tbsp pine nuts

3 Tbsp avocado or olive oil

1 head cauliflower, about 1¾ lb [800 g], trimmed and cut into florets

Pinch of kosher salt

1 tsp chopped garlic

1 tsp finely chopped shallot

1 tsp chopped fresh chives

1 tsp grated lemon zest

1½ limes, cut into halves

½ tsp red pepper flakes

2 Tbsp chopped fresh basil

3 Tbsp chopped fresh cilantro

3 Tbsp chopped fresh mint

3 Tbsp plain yogurt

½ tsp honey

¼ tsp ground sumac

¼ tsp flaky sea salt

Heat the oven to 425°F [220°C].

Toast the pine nuts in a small, dry frying pan over medium-high heat, stirring frequently, until browned, about 2 minutes. Remove from the heat and set aside.

Heat the oil in a large cast-iron sauté pan or frying pan over medium-high heat until hot and shimmering. Add the cauliflower and sprinkle with a pinch of salt. Sear the cauliflower, tossing or stirring occasionally, until the edges are browned, 2 to 3 minutes.

Transfer the cauliflower to the oven and cook until tender, about 15 minutes.

Carefully return the pan to the stove over medium-high heat. Add the garlic, shallot, chives, and lemon zest and cook, stirring, just until the garlic is fragrant, about 1 minute. Remove from the heat. Squeeze the juice from 1 lime over the top and gently stir in the pepper flakes, toasted pine nuts, basil, cilantro, and mint. Transfer to a platter or serving bowl.

Put the yogurt in a small bowl. Squeeze the juice from the remaining ½ lime over the top and stir in the honey. Drizzle the honeyed yogurt over the cauliflower and sprinkle with the sumac and flaky sea salt. Serve immediately.

Sautéed broccolini with Mexican sriracha and queso fresco

Queso fresco and sriracha might seem like an odd match for broccolini, but the spicy, umami-rich Mexican sriracha and mild fresh cheese are delicious with earthy vegetables. Thin-stemmed broccolini is a hybrid of broccoli and gai lan (leafy Chinese broccoli). Originally developed in Japan as Aspabroc, it has notes of both broccoli and asparagus and is slightly sweet and earthy and grassy. This is a go-to side vegetable with roasts like prime rib or rack of lamb but also something I'll wrap up in a warm griddled tortilla or flatbread and eat with my hands.

SERVES 4

1 Tbsp avocado or olive oil

2 bunches broccolini, about 1 lb [455 g], trimmed

¼ tsp salt

½ lime

2 Tbsp Mexican sriracha (page 85)

2 Tbsp crumbled queso fresco

Heat the oil in a frying pan or grill pan over medium-high heat until hot and shimmering. Add the broccolini, sprinkle with the salt, and sear until the edges are browned, about 2 minutes on each side. Remove from the heat and transfer to a platter. Squeeze the juice from the lime over the broccolini, drizzle with the Mexican sriracha, and garnish with the crumbled queso fresco. Serve immediately.

Baked fenugreek-nigella pork and beef meatballs

This recipe makes a baking sheet full of tender, flavorful meatballs spiced with nigella, fenugreek, and Aleppo pepper, along with a little miso. Mix the ingredients as gently as possible so that the meatballs are tender and light. Use them in sandwiches, for tomato-dill pappardelle with caraway bread crumbs (page 169), or serve them sautéed with bitter greens such as Tuscan kale (page 137). The fenugreek and nigella in these meatballs are especially savory, but I often switch up the seasoning, using the spice mixture berberé instead (see variation), or a few spoonfuls of chimichurri (page 84), or both.

MAKES 19 MEATBALLS

1 Tbsp coriander seeds

⅓ cup [80 ml] whole milk

⅓ cup [80 g] white miso

2 eggs

½ cup [60 g] grated Pecorino cheese

3 Tbsp dried fenugreek leaves

1 Tbsp nigella seeds

1 Tbsp finely chopped garlic

2 tsp sweet paprika

2 tsp Aleppo pepper

½ tsp salt

⅓ cup [35 g] caraway bread crumbs (page 54) or ⅓ cup [40 g] panko

1 lb [455 g] ground beef

1 lb [455 g] ground pork

Heat the oven to 400°F [200°C]. Line a baking sheet with parchment paper.

Toast the coriander seeds in a small, dry frying pan over medium heat, stirring occasionally, until fragrant, 1 to 2 minutes. Grind the seeds to a fine powder in a spice grinder or with a mortar and pestle. Set aside.

Whisk together the milk, miso, and eggs in a medium bowl. Add the Pecorino cheese, fenugreek, nigella, garlic, paprika, Aleppo pepper, ground coriander, and salt and mix thoroughly. Whisk in the bread crumbs.

cont'd

Gently mix the beef and pork with the milk-miso-and-egg mixture with your hands, or with one hand and a rubber spatula, being careful not to overwork the mixture.

Form the meat mixture into golf ball–size meatballs (2½ oz [70 g] each), gently rolling them into spheres with your hands. Arrange the meatballs on the parchment-lined baking sheet (they release a lot of juices).

Bake until the internal temperature reaches 155°F [70°C] on an instant-read thermometer, 20 to 25 minutes. Use immediately, for pasta, sandwiches, or with vegetables such as the Tuscan kale with crushed fenugreek-nigella meatballs and sherry raisins (facing page), or store them in a covered container in the refrigerator for up to 2 days.

VARIATION

Berberé-spiced meatballs: Omit the coriander, dried fenugreek leaves, nigella, paprika, and Aleppo pepper. Stir in 1 Tbsp berberé (page 36) with the Pecorino, garlic, and salt. Add ¼ cup [60 g] currants and ¼ cup [35 g] pine nuts with the pork and beef.

Tuscan kale with crushed fenugreek-nigella meatballs and sherry raisins

With its dark blue-green color, embossed leaves, and rich, earthy flavor, Tuscan kale (also known as lacinato) is my favorite type of kale. It's more delicate and slightly sweeter than other varieties. Here, I blanch/wilt the leaves before I do anything else with them, to nudge them toward that almost creamy texture. (An easy way to "blanch" them: Put trimmed leaves in a colander in the kitchen sink and pour boiling water over them.) You won't get the same texture if you sauté raw leaves. This dish combines earthy kale and radishes with spiced meatballs that have a lot of heady flavors. Raisins soaked in sherry are pungent and nutty and not too sweet. You can make extra raisins for pouring over ice cream or adding to other desserts such as bread pudding.

NOTE: The sherry raisins should soak for at least 1 hour. (They can be stored in their liquid, covered and refrigerated, for up to a month.)

SERVES 4

½ cup [120 ml] dry sherry, preferably good-quality fino or amontillado

1 dried arbol chile

¼ cup [50 g] golden raisins

4 bunches Tuscan kale, about 1½ lb [680 g] total, center ribs removed

3 Tbsp avocado or olive oil

8 French breakfast radishes, halved lengthwise

2 garlic cloves, sliced

¼ tsp salt

1 recipe baked fenugreek-nigella pork and beef meatballs (page 135), broken into large pieces

1 tsp finely chopped shallot

1 tsp finely chopped fresh chives

1 tsp grated lemon zest

Fresh black pepper

1 lemon, halved

½ Tbsp urfa biber shichimi togarashi (page 38) or toasted white sesame seeds (optional)

Put the sherry and arbol chile in a saucepan and bring to a gentle simmer over low heat; any flames will dissipate after 30 to 45 seconds (do not use high heat, as it will burn off the alcohol). Add the raisins and simmer for 1 minute. Remove from the heat, discard the chile, and set aside. Let the raisins soak for at least 1 hour before using.

cont'd

Bring a large pot of salted water to a boil over high heat. Put the kale leaves in a large heatproof colander and set the colander in your kitchen sink. Carefully pour the boiling water over the leaves. Run cold water over the kale until it's cool enough to handle, then gently squeeze the leaves to remove as much of the remaining water as possible. After a gentle wringing, you will end up with a log-shaped bundle of kale. Cut the kale crosswise into 3-in [7.5-cm] sections, gently pulling the leaves apart with your fingers. Set aside.

Heat 2 Tbsp of the oil in a large sauté pan over medium-high heat until hot and shimmering. Add the radishes and sauté, stirring occasionally, until they have caramelized and are cooked through but still have crunch, 3 to 5 minutes. Add the chopped blanched kale and sauté until warmed through, about 2 minutes.

Clear a small area along one side of the pan to cook the garlic. Add the remaining 1 Tbsp oil and the garlic; as soon as the garlic starts to sizzle, stir it into the kale mixture so that it doesn't burn. Add the salt, meatballs, shallot, chives, lemon zest, and a few grinds of black pepper. Give it a stir and remove the pan from the heat.

Transfer to a platter. Squeeze the juice from the lemon over the kale mixture. Drain the sherry raisins and sprinkle over the top, along with the shichimi togarashi, if desired. Serve immediately.

Texture is one of the most vital elements of a dish: creamy, crunchy, snappy, juicy, fatty, tender. Of these and more, crispy is a singular experience. There's nothing else like that initial shattering crackle when you bite into crispy hash browns, fritters, schnitzel, or layers of flaky phyllo. It's why I love panko-crusted tonkatsu (Japanese pork cutlets); the pointiest tip of a baguette *bien cuit* ("well cooked"), which the French sometimes call *le croûton*; and fritto misto with the thinnest layer of fried batter.

But I might like crispy even better when it is paired with something creamy and cool. Or when something like buttery, golden, flaky bread crumbs are an accent for a pile of fresh greens and herbs, a platter of carpaccio, or sprinkled on top of a bowl of supple pasta or nutty whole grains.

A signature dish at Bäco Mercat is the hamachi crudo with crushed avocado and potato croquette. Crudo of raw Japanese amberjack comes with a fried potato croquette that is crispy and golden on the outside and tender on the inside. So you taste cool fish (dressed with adjika, yuzu, and dashi) with creamy avocado and the fried crunch of the potato fritter's exterior. It's a study in contrasts that all comes together as a balance of flavors, temperatures, and textures.

The best and most efficient way I know to achieve the ultimate crispiness is heat and fat. (Also, "Fat gives things flavor," as Julia Child said.) Hot oil transfers heat much more quickly than does hot air in an oven. Baking and roasting can result in crispiness, too—the very edges of a brownie, the crackling skin of a whole roast duck. Frying is just a lot faster because the liquid fat delivers heat to even the smallest crevices on the surface of the food.

Of course, nature delivers crisp textures, too. I think of fresh jicama, radishes, lettuces such as romaine, Honeycrisp apple (the crispest of the crisp apples), and Asian pear.

But don't be afraid to fry. It's a great, efficient way to cook something quickly with standout results: a lot of complex flavor, golden-brown color, and delicious texture.

For bright contrast to fried foods, the classic standby is tangy-fresh lemon (I also like yuzu), its juice squeezed from wedges all over fried chicken, calamari, or chicharrones. Or use spicy hot sauces or lots of herbs. I like the explosion of crispiness with a hit of freshness from parsley, chives, or celery leaves.

buttery

crispy

CHAPTER

4

rangy

herbal

Griddled corn cake with aonori mascarpone butter

This griddled corn cake is a version of johnnycake, originally an unleavened bread of cornmeal, salt, and water made by Native Americans. Made with polenta and buttermilk, it has a buttery crisp crust, especially around the edges, with a soft and fluffy interior. I use polenta because it is made from a specific variety of Italian corn and is milled differently than cornmeal, for a fuller texture. The corn cake is topped with homemade butter folded with the soft Italian cheese mascarpone and aonori (ground Japanese seaweed). I like the nutty, toasty corn flavor of the griddle cake with the sweet creaminess of mascarpone and the grassy, tea-like flavor of aonori. You can also make smaller pancakes (variation follows).

NOTE: Anson Mills coarse-ground polenta is available online.

MAKES 3 GRIDDLE CAKES (EACH SERVES 2)

1 cup [165 g] coarse-ground polenta, preferably Anson Mills Coarse Rustic Polenta Integrale

½ cup plus 1 Tbsp [70 g] all-purpose flour

½ cup plus 1 Tbsp [70 g] pastry flour

3 Tbsp sugar

1 tsp kosher salt

½ tsp baking soda

¼ tsp baking powder

1 cup [240 ml] buttermilk

2 Tbsp honey

2 eggs

½ cup [110 g] butter, melted and cooled

3 Tbsp butter or ghee (page 86) for cooking

6 Tbsp aonori mascarpone butter (page 88) for serving

Flaky sea salt

Heat the oven to 400°F [200°C].

Whisk together the polenta, all-purpose flour, pastry flour, sugar, salt, baking soda, and baking powder in a large bowl. Add the buttermilk, honey, eggs, and melted and cooled butter and stir until combined. If not using right away, store in a covered container in the refrigerator for up to 2 days.

cont'd

Heat 1 Tbsp of the butter in a 6-in [15-cm] cast-iron frying pan over medium-high heat until foaming and melted, but not brown. Swirl the pan so that the butter covers the bottom. Ladle about 1 cup [225 g] batter into the pan. Carefully but quickly spread it evenly with a spatula to the sides of the pan. Cook the griddle cake until a browned crust forms on the bottom and bubbles form on the top, about 2 minutes. Transfer to the oven and bake until set and the top looks dry, about 10 minutes.

Carefully return the pan to the stove over medium-high heat and flip the cake, cooking the second side until golden brown, about 2 minutes. You can serve this in the pan immediately. Or transfer to a platter, loosely tent with aluminum foil, and set aside. Repeat with the remaining batter and butter to make 2 more griddle cakes.

Top each griddle cake with 2 Tbsp aonori mascarpone butter and sprinkle with sea salt to taste. Serve immediately.

VARIATION

Griddled corn pancakes with aonori mascarpone butter: Make the batter as directed in the preceding recipe. Heat 1 tsp butter in a large frying pan over medium-high heat until foaming and melted, but not brown. Swirl the pan so that the butter covers the bottom. Ladle batter into the pan, making pancakes any size you like. Adjust the heat as necessary (you usually need higher heat for the first batch). Cook the pancakes until a browned crust forms on the bottoms and bubbles form on the top, about 2 minutes. Flip and cook the second side until golden brown, about 2 minutes. Transfer to a plate or platter, loosely tent with foil, and repeat with the remaining batter. Serve immediately with aonori mascarpone butter (page 88) or transfer to a plate and keep warm in a 200°F [95°C] oven for up to 15 minutes.

Jicama salad with mango, fennel, cucumber, peanuts, and lime and fish sauce vinaigrette

Jicama is a sweet, nutty root vegetable originating from Mexico; it has also been called Mexican water chestnut because of its crisp white flesh. This salad is a riff on a traditional preparation of chilled jicama and mango slices with chile, salt, and lime, crossed with Southeast Asian papaya salad. Other crunchy vegetables, along with peanuts, herbs, and tropical mango, lend a lot of flavors and textures.

SERVES 4 TO 6

1 large jicama, about 2 lb [910 g]
2 mangoes
6 to 8 small red radishes
½ fennel bulb
1 cucumber
1 cup [14 g] fresh cilantro leaves
1 cup [16 g] fresh mint leaves
½ cup [70 g] peanuts
1 serrano chile, cut into thin slices
¼ cup [60 ml] lime and fish sauce vinaigrette (page 71)

Peel the jicama with a vegetable peeler or sharp knife and cut it in half. Julienne the jicama by cutting each half into ⅛-in [3-mm] slices, then lay each slice flat and cut into ⅛-in- [3-mm-] wide batons. Transfer to a large bowl and set aside.

Peel the mangoes with a vegetable peeler. Cut lengthwise (parallel to the widest side of the pit) into ⅛-in [3-mm] slices and discard the pits. Lay each slice flat and cut into ⅛-in- [3-mm-] wide batons. Add to the bowl with the jicama. Julienne the radishes into ⅛-in- [3-mm-] wide batons and add to the bowl.

Cut the fennel into very thin slices with a mandoline, then lay each slice flat and cut into ¼-in- [6-mm-] wide batons. Add to the bowl. Cut the cucumber in half lengthwise; scoop out the seeds with a spoon and discard. Thinly slice the cucumber halves on the bias. Add to the bowl.

Add the cilantro, mint, peanuts, serrano chile, and vinaigrette to the bowl and gently toss together. Transfer to a platter and serve immediately.

Panko-crusted shrimp with chives and Mexican sriracha

These crispy butterflied shrimp are golden brown and crackling on the out-side, tender on the inside, and great for dipping into spicy, tangy Mexican sriracha. The sriracha—which has the bright heat of arbol chiles, the acidity of vinegar, the aromatics of garlic and shallots, and the umami of fish sauce—is an excellent partner for the fried shrimp. I might also dunk them into chimichurri. You can also serve the shrimp folded inside fluffy-soft flatbread (page 176) along with the hot sauce and a crunchy cabbage slaw (page 102) for a sandwich.

SERVES 4

12 shell-on jumbo shrimp (16 to 20 per pound)
⅔ cup [80 g] flour
1 tsp kosher salt
2 eggs, lightly beaten
2 cups [240 g] panko
Avocado or light olive oil for frying
Flaky sea salt
1 bunch chives, cut into 2-in [5-cm] lengths
½ cup [120 ml] Mexican sriracha (page 85)

Peel the shrimp, discarding the shells and legs. Devein the shrimp by cutting along the back with a sharp paring knife and removing the dark vein with the tip of the knife. To butterfly the shrimp, cut along the same cut to make a deeper incision, but don't cut all the way through the shrimp. Now you will be able to open up the shrimp so that it's nearly flat. (I don't like to cut too deeply, making it too flat; I like the shrimp to have a little bit of shape.) Place the shrimp in a colander and rinse with cold water; give the colander a good shake to remove any excess water. Pat the shrimp dry with paper towels and set aside.

cont'd

Mix the flour and salt together with a fork or whisk in a medium bowl. Put the eggs in another bowl, and the panko in a third bowl. Using one hand, place a few shrimp at a time in the flour to lightly coat them. With the other hand, gently dip them into the beaten egg, shaking off any excess, then toss the shrimp in the panko so that they are evenly coated. (Uncurl the shrimp and make sure there are no clumps of panko in any creases.) Set aside on a plate. Repeat with the remaining shrimp.

Line a plate with paper towels. Pour enough oil into a medium saucepan to come up the sides about 3 in [7.5 cm]. Heat the oil over medium-high heat until it reaches 375°F [190°C] on a candy or deep-fry thermometer. (You can also insert the handle of a wooden spoon into the oil so that it touches the bottom of the pan. Look for small bubbles that come up the sides of the spoon, indicating that the oil is hot enough.)

Fry the shrimp in two batches. Using metal tongs, carefully place the shrimp, one at a time, into the hot oil. Swirl the tongs in the oil as the shrimp cook, touching them with the tong ends—these are like an extension of your fingers and you'll learn to "feel" the shrimp getting crispy. When the shrimp are light golden brown, after 1 to 2 minutes, remove them with the tongs and place on the paper towel–lined plate to drain (by the time you've set them on the paper towels, they will have turned a nice medium golden brown). Fry the remaining shrimp. Sprinkle with flaky sea salt to taste.

Transfer the shrimp to a platter, sprinkle with the chives, and serve immediately with a side of Mexican sriracha.

Potato croquettes

At Bäco Mercat, these potato croquettes are served with hamachi crudo, accented with adjika, yuzu, and dashi (recipe follows). When fried, they develop a thin crispy-crackly crust, while inside they are all tender potato. The addition of cheddar is a flavor boost (but only a little is added; otherwise, they can fall apart). They're also great as hash browns, alongside cheesy scrambled eggs and jamón ibérico, or as a side dish or an appetizer, to dunk into chimichurri or salsa verde or any hot sauce.

MAKES 12 CROQUETTES

2 russet potatoes, about 1¼ lb [570 g] total, scrubbed but not peeled
1 egg yolk
½ tsp garlic powder
½ tsp onion powder
¼ cup [20 g] grated aged white cheddar
½ tsp cornstarch
½ tsp kosher salt
Fresh black pepper
Avocado or olive oil for frying
Flaky sea salt

Heat the oven to 400°F [200°C].

Prick the potatoes all over with the tines of a fork. Place them directly on an oven rack. Bake, rotating the potatoes halfway through, until the potatoes give slightly when squeezed, like a slightly underripe avocado, 45 to 50 minutes. They should not be too soft or the texture inside the croquettes will be dense rather than light and fluffy.

While the potatoes are still hot, very carefully peel them using a paring knife; discard the skins. Carefully grate the potatoes on the large holes of a box grater into a large bowl.

Add the egg yolk, garlic powder, onion powder, cheddar, cornstarch, kosher salt, and a few grinds of black pepper and mix by hand until well combined.

Form the mixture into 12 golf ball–size fritters (about 1¼ oz [35 g] each), rolling them into spheres with your hands. Lightly moisten your hands as needed if the potato mixture sticks.

cont'd

Line a plate with paper towels. Pour enough oil into a small pot to come up the sides about 2 in [5 cm]. Heat the oil over medium-high heat until it reaches 350°F [180°C] on a candy or deep-fry thermometer. Using a skimmer, carefully place three or four potato croquettes into the hot oil. Fry until golden brown, 3 to 4 minutes. Remove the croquettes with the skimmer and place on the paper towel–lined plate to drain. Continue to fry the remaining croquettes, a few at a time.

Transfer to a platter, sprinkle with sea salt to taste, and serve immediately. Or, if you're making hamachi crudo (page 154), transfer the croquettes to a baking sheet and keep warm in a 200°F [95°C] oven for up to 30 minutes.

Hamachi crudo with adjika, yuzu-dashi vinaigrette, avocado, and potato croquettes

This dish has evolved over several years, as it has been tweaked and tweaked and tweaked again—now it's a signature dish at Bäco Mercat. It started as sashimi of hamachi (amberjack) garnished with gremolata and bacon as part of a tasting menu. Over time, the sashimi became crudo, and the bacon and gremolata were replaced with yuzu juice and dashi. Adjika (the spicy pepper sauce of Abkhazia and Georgia; pictured on page 156), punctuated by herbs and chiles, was added later. The avocado adds melt-in-your-mouth creaminess, a nice contrast to the crispy potato croquette.

NOTE: See the note on page 122 about bottled shiro dashi, which can be substituted for the dashi concentrate. High-quality bottled yuzu juice is available at Japanese markets and online. Tonburi is the seed of the Japanese broom cypress tree. Sometimes called land caviar, the seeds are used as a garnish for their nutty, earthy (quinoa-like) flavor. The jarred seeds are available at select Japanese markets and online.

SERVES 4

10 oz [280 g] sashimi-grade hamachi (amberjack) or yellowtail fillets, cut into large dice

3 tsp dashi concentrate (page 76)

3 tsp yuzu juice

1 Tbsp olive oil

1 tsp finely chopped shallot

1 tsp finely chopped fresh chives

1 tsp grated lemon zest

1 tsp tonburi (optional)

1 ripe avocado, peeled, pitted, and cut into large dice

1 tsp fresh lime juice

½ tsp kosher salt

Fresh black pepper

2 Tbsp adjika vinaigrette (page 64)

8 to 12 potato croquettes (page 151), kept warm

2 Tbsp crème fraîche (page 94)

Several pale celery leaves for garnish

Flaky sea salt

cont'd

Gently mix the hamachi, dashi concentrate, yuzu juice, and olive oil in a large bowl. Mix the shallot, chives, and lemon zest in a small bowl and add 2 tsp of the mixture to the seasoned hamachi. Gently stir the tonburi (if using) into the hamachi mixture. Set aside.

In another bowl, gently mix the avocado, lime juice, salt, several grinds of black pepper, and the remaining 1 tsp shallot-chive-zest mixture.

Divide the hamachi mixture among four plates. Drizzle the adjika vinaigrette over the hamachi mixture, dividing it evenly. Divide the avocado mixture among the four plates, placing it next to the hamachi. Place 2 or 3 potato croquettes on each plate alongside the hamachi and avocado, slightly crushing the croquettes with a fork. Dollop the crème fraîche on top of the hamachi and add a few celery leaves. Sprinkle each dish with a pinch of sea salt. Serve immediately.

Coffee-rubbed beef carpaccio with juniper-tarragon vinaigrette and crispy shallots

The coffee and warm spices of one of my favorite rubs for meat and a botanical-meets-briny juniper-tarragon vinaigrette work together to bring a lot of flavors to beefy carpaccio. I think a platter of carpaccio is kind of spectacular, and it's easy to make. Just start with great meat, preferably grass-fed. You can use any lean cut of meat such as top round, but I prefer tenderloin or even petite tender, which is a butcher's cut (i.e., not as popular and therefore typically, or theoretically, less expensive) from the shoulder. Crispy-fried shallots are always a good idea.

SERVES 4

One 8-oz [230-g] beef shoulder petite tender or tenderloin

½ tsp salt

1 tsp coffee-spice rub (page 40)

1 Tbsp avocado or olive oil, plus oil for frying

1 Tbsp butter

1 garlic clove, peeled

1 sprig thyme

1 sprig rosemary

1 fresh bay leaf (optional)

2 shallots, cut into thin slices

1 to 2 Tbsp juniper-tarragon vinaigrette (page 72), or as needed

Fresh black pepper

2 Tbsp shaved Parmigiano-Reggiano

Handful of celery leaves for garnish

Sprinkle the beef with the salt, followed by the coffee rub, making sure the beef is evenly coated on all sides. Set aside.

Heat 1 Tbsp of the oil in a small frying pan over high heat until hot and shimmering. Carefully add the beef to the pan using metal tongs. When the beef is seared on one side (it will be a very dark brown because of the coffee rub), about 30 seconds, give it a quarter turn and add the butter, garlic, thyme, rosemary, and bay leaf (if using). Baste the meat with the butter and continue to turn the beef as it sears, about 30 seconds per side. (You're just searing the outside; the beef should otherwise be raw.) When all of the sides have been seared, transfer the beef to a plate. Discard the garlic, herb sprigs, and bay leaf. Cover the beef in plastic wrap, refrigerate, and cool completely, 1½ to 2 hours.

cont'd

Line a plate with paper towels. Pour enough oil into a small saucepan to come up the sides about 1 in [2.5 cm]. Heat the oil over medium-high heat until hot and shimmering. Check that the oil is hot enough by adding a slice or two of shallot; it should sizzle. Using a slotted spoon, carefully place the shallots into the hot oil. Fry, stirring occasionally, until golden brown and crispy, 8 to 10 minutes. Remove the shallots with the slotted spoon and place on the paper towel–lined plate to drain. Set aside.

Remove the beef from the refrigerator and cut it into very thin slices, between ⅛ and ¼ in [3 and 6 mm] thick. Lay a sheet of plastic wrap on a flat surface. Place the beef slices in a single layer on the plastic wrap, with at least 1 to 2 in [2.5 to 5 cm] between the slices because the meat will spread once you pound it. Top with another piece of plastic wrap. Gently pound the meat with a mallet (or even a small heavy-bottomed saucepan) until paper-thin. Repeat until all of the meat is pounded.

Arrange the beef slices on a serving platter and drizzle with the vinaigrette. Sprinkle with several grinds of black pepper, the Parmigiano-Reggiano, the fried shallots, and celery leaves. Serve immediately.

Panfried rainbow trout with brown butter, Meyer lemon, green olives, and chives

Rainbow trout is delicate and flaky, its lean meat a great match for rich brown butter balanced with lots of Meyer lemon and briny-fruity green olives. The flavors remind me of a North African tagine of chicken braised with lemons and olives—but it's much quicker cooking, and the edges of the fish get nicely browned and crispy. Serve it with couscous tossed with herbs and topped with butter, a little piment d'Espelette, and orange zest, or with a crisp salad of kale, shaved fennel, cauliflower, and apple (page 113).

NOTE: You can ask at the fish counter for your trout to be scaled, dressed, and butterflied. You can use ¼ cup [60 g] Curry leaf Meyer lemon pickle (page 26) instead of the Meyer lemon slices. Top the fish with the lemon pickle after pouring over the brown butter and Meyer lemon juice.

SERVES 2 TO 4

2 whole rainbow trout, about 8 oz [230 g] each, scaled and butterflied
Salt
Fresh black pepper
2 Tbsp avocado or olive oil
5 Tbsp [75 g] butter, cut into slices
1 Meyer lemon, cut into thin slices
Juice of 1 Meyer lemon
¼ cup [35 g] green olives, preferably Castelvetrano
½ cup [28 g] chopped fresh chives

Pat the trout dry, inside and out, with paper towels and season the flesh side of each butterflied fish with 1 pinch of salt and 2 grinds of black pepper. Set aside.

Heat 1 Tbsp of the oil in a large heavy-bottomed frying pan over medium-high heat until hot and shimmering. Carefully place one trout in the pan, skin side down, and sear (slightly tilting the pan now and then to ensure even oil distribution) until the skin has crisped and the fish becomes opaque at the edges, 2 to 3 minutes. Very carefully turn the fish over with a spatula and cook the other side just until lightly browned, 30 to 40 seconds. Transfer to a platter, skin side up, and let rest.

cont'd

Carefully wipe the pan clean with a paper towel and repeat for the second trout, adding the remaining 1 Tbsp oil to the pan. Transfer to the same platter and let rest (also skin side up). Wipe the pan clean again.

Return the pan to medium heat. Add the butter and cook, whisking frequently, until the milk solids begin to brown, 1 to 2 minutes. It will first foam a little, then subside, and lightly browned specks will form at the bottom of the pan (there should be a nutty aroma, but watch that it doesn't burn). Add the Meyer lemon slices and juice, remove from the heat, and set aside.

Flip the trout on the platter so that they are skin side down. Pour the brown butter and lemons over the fish. Sprinkle with the olives and chives. Serve immediately.

Citrus and dry-cured olive salad

A salad of oranges with dry-cured black olives is a particularly Moroccan dish that recalls the orange and olive trees of Agadir and Essaouira along the coast. This salad combines sautéed shallots, warmed olives, and fresh citrus—oranges, grapefruits, and lemons. You can mix up the citrus, using blood oranges or Cara Cara oranges or clementines, or sour oranges such as Seville or bergamot instead of lemon. It's especially attractive with garlic or chive blossoms when you can find them. I like to serve it with lightly cured ocean trout (page 166); grilled or panfried fish; and roast chicken, beef, or lamb.

NOTE: Oil- or dry-cured black olives, such as Beldi, Nyon, or Thassos, are available at select markets and online.

SERVES 4

3 grapefruits

3 oranges

3 lemons

1 Tbsp avocado or olive oil

2 shallots, cut into very thin slices

¼ cup [40 g] oil- or dry-cured black olives

Pinch of kosher salt

½ bunch parsley, leaves only

1½ Tbsp extra-virgin olive oil

Pinch of flaky sea salt

Fresh black pepper

TO SEGMENT THE GRAPEFRUITS: Trim a little off the top and bottom of each grapefruit with a sharp knife so that there are two flat ends. Set a grapefruit flat on a cutting surface and cut away the peel and white skin from top to bottom, working your way around the fruit. Remove each citrus segment by cutting between the fruit and the membrane for each section; the wedges should release easily. Transfer to a medium bowl. Repeat with the oranges, remaining grapefruits, and lemons and transfer to the same bowl. Set aside.

cont'd

Line a plate with paper towels. Heat the avocado oil in a frying pan over high heat until hot and shimmering. Carefully add the shallots and cook, stirring continuously, until the shallots are caramelized and dark golden brown, about 2 minutes. During the last 30 seconds of cooking, add the olives. Remove from the heat and transfer the shallots and olives to the paper towel–lined plate. Sprinkle with a pinch of kosher salt and set aside.

Add the parsley and olive oil to the citrus segments, followed by the shallots and olives. Mix gently and sprinkle with a pinch of flaky sea salt and a few grinds of black pepper. Transfer to a platter and serve immediately.

Slow-roasted berberé-cured ocean trout with lemon tempura and citrus and olive salad

Just-fatty-enough mild ocean trout is lightly cured with this mixture of sugar, salt, and Ethiopian berberé. Heavy on the Aleppo pepper, fenugreek leaves, paprika, and cubeb pepper, berberé makes a good curing spice, imparting its complex, warm flavors and aromas. Slow-roasting is an ideal way to cook ocean trout; it brings out the best in its texture—meaty but delicate, silky and supple. The fish can be cured in advance. And while it's slow-roasting, you'll have time to make a light salad and tempura-battered, thinly sliced lemon that is crispy, tart, and juicy all at once.

SERVES 4 TO 6

3 Tbsp sugar

3 Tbsp salt

1½ Tbsp berberé (page 36)

One 1½-lb [680-g] ocean trout fillet

1½ Tbsp avocado or olive oil, plus more for frying

¾ cup [90 g] flour

⅔ cup [80 g] cornstarch

1 tsp baking soda

1 tsp kosher salt

1¼ cups [300 ml] ice-cold sparkling water

1 lemon, cut into ⅛-in [3-mm] slices using a mandoline

2 scallions, green parts only, cut into thin slices on the bias

1½ tsp extra-virgin olive oil

Flaky sea salt

Fresh black pepper or Aleppo pepper

1 recipe citrus and dry-cured olive salad (page 163)

Mix the sugar, salt, and berberé on a large plate. Place the ocean trout on the plate and turn to evenly coat the fish on all sides with the sugar-salt-spice mixture. Set a rack over a rimmed baking sheet, put the fish on the rack, and cover tightly with plastic wrap. Cure in the refrigerator for 1 hour, then rinse and pat completely dry with paper towels. The fish can be prepared in advance and refrigerated for up to 1 day.

cont'd

Heat the oven to 200°F [95°C]. Remove the fish from the refrigerator and rub it with the 1½ Tbsp avocado oil. Return the fish to the rack set over the baking sheet and transfer to the oven. Roast until the fish is cooked through and meltingly tender, about 50 minutes. When you press gently on the fillet, its segments should separate easily. Remove the trout from the oven and set aside to cool for 15 minutes.

MAKE THE LEMON TEMPURA: Whisk together the flour, cornstarch, baking soda, kosher salt, and sparkling water in a large bowl to make a thin batter. The batter should coat the back of a spoon and have a nappe consistency (if you run your finger along the back of the coated spoon, you should see a clean line).

Line a plate with paper towels. Pour enough avocado oil into a sauce-pan to come up the sides about 2 in [5 cm]. Heat the oil over medium-high heat until it reaches 375°F [190°C] on a candy or deep-fry thermometer. Dip the lemon slices, one at a time, into the batter and gently shake off any excess. As soon as you dip a lemon slice into the batter, use a fork or chopsticks to carefully place it into the hot oil. Fry the lemon slices, a few at a time, carefully flipping them once during cooking, until golden brown, about 1 minute on each side. Remove the lemon slices with the fork or chopsticks and place on the paper towel–lined plate to drain. Set aside.

Gently flip the cooled trout over and peel and discard the skin. Gently scrape away the gray bloodline using a spoon. With the spoon, separate the fillet into large chunks along its segments.

Transfer the trout to a platter. Scatter the scallions on top, drizzle with the extra-virgin olive oil, and sprinkle with flaky sea salt to taste and a couple of grinds of black pepper or a pinch of Aleppo pepper. Put the lemon tempura and the citrus and olive salad on the same platter alongside the trout. Serve immediately.

Tomato-dill pappardelle with caraway bread crumbs

Dill isn't one of the usual herb suspects for tomato sauce; those would be oregano and basil. But I like its sweet, citrusy, tangy flavor with the brightness of tomatoes. Dill is in the celery family, which might be why I like it so much (I'm a fan of just about all things celery). The buttery-crispy bread crumbs are spiced with garlic, thyme, and caraway. I also might sprinkle a little berberé (page 36) over my pasta.

NOTE: This recipe makes more tomato-dill sauce than you need for the pappardelle. Store in a covered container in the refrigerator for up to 3 days. Use it for any pasta.

SERVES 4

1 Tbsp olive oil

1 small red onion, grated

6 garlic cloves, cut into thin slices

⅛ tsp red pepper flakes

¼ cup [60 ml] dry white wine

One 28-oz [794-g] can whole tomatoes, crushed by hand, with their juice

1 tsp sherry vinegar

¼ tsp salt

8 to 10 fresh basil leaves, torn

1 tsp chopped dill fronds, plus more for garnish

1 recipe pappardelle (page 203)

¼ to ½ cup [25 to 50 g] caraway bread crumbs (page 54)

Pecorino Romano, for grating

Heat the oil in a heavy-bottomed frying pan over medium-high heat until hot and shimmering. Add the onion, garlic, and red pepper flakes and cook, stirring occasionally, until the onion begins to brown, 3 to 5 minutes. Remove from the heat and add the wine. Return the pan to medium-high heat and cook for 1 minute so that the flavors meld.

Add the tomatoes with their juice, sherry vinegar, and salt. Lower the heat and simmer, stirring occasionally, until slightly reduced, 12 to 15 minutes. Remove from the heat and stir in the basil and 1 tsp dill. You should have about 3 cups [710 ml]. Keep warm on the stove, or cool and store in a covered container in the refrigerator for up to 3 days.

cont'd

Bring a pot of salted water to a boil over high heat. Add the pappardelle and cook until al dente, 2 to 3 minutes. Drain the pasta. Divide the pasta among four plates and top with the desired amount of tomato-dill sauce. Garnish with a little bit of extra dill. Top each plate with 1 or 2 Tbsp bread crumbs, but only just before serving so that they stay crispy. Serve immediately, passing the Pecorino Romano.

Lengua "schnitzel" with brown butter, capers, and cherry tomatoes

Lengua (beef tongue) might not immediately come to mind when you're thinking about schnitzel, the Austrian dish traditionally made with thinly pounded veal, coated with flour, egg, and bread crumbs, and then fried. But I love tender braised tongue prepared much the same way, so that it has a crisp-crackly crust (here, it's panko) that contrasts with the delicate meat. It's true that tongue requires some special handling, but I think its texture and flavor are unmatched. The closest comparison might be mild brisket. The lengua is first braised with lots of aromatics, then sliced into cutlets. These are dipped in egg and panko, then panfried. Cutlets of panko-crusted lengua are the filling for one of the Bäco sandwiches at Bäco Mercat, with several sliced pickles, harissa, and smoked paprika aioli. Here, it's sauced with salty, tangy capers and tomatoes enriched with nutty brown butter.

NOTE: I recommend braising and chilling the meat a day in advance.

SERVES 4

1 lb [455 g] lengua (beef tongue)

1 Tbsp berberé (page 36)

1 large carrot, cut into large pieces

1 yellow onion, cut into large pieces

2 celery stalks, cut into large pieces

1 head garlic, halved crosswise

1 sprig rosemary

1 sprig thyme

1 dried bay leaf

Salt

⅓ cup [40 g] flour

2 eggs, lightly beaten

2 cups [240 g] panko

¼ cup [60 ml] avocado or olive oil

2 Tbsp butter

Juice of ½ lemon

1 Tbsp capers

8 cherry tomatoes, halved

1 Tbsp dried fenugreek leaves

1 tsp urfa biber or 1 pinch of cayenne pepper (optional)

½ cup [8 g] fresh mint leaves

Heat the oven to 350°F [180°C].

To blanch the lengua, fill a large pot or Dutch oven with water, add the lengua, and bring to a boil over high heat. Lower the heat and simmer for 5 minutes. Drain, rinse, then pat dry with paper towels. Coat the meat evenly with the berberé and place it back in the pot or Dutch oven.

Wrap the carrot, onion, celery, garlic, rosemary, thyme, and bay leaf in a large piece of cheesecloth and tie it together with kitchen string. Place the wrapped vegetables on top of the lengua. Fill the pot with enough water to cover the meat, add a pinch of salt, and bring it to a boil over high heat. Remove from the heat, cover the pot, and carefully transfer it to the oven. Braise until tender, about 2 hours; a knife or skewer inserted into the tongue should pierce it easily.

Discard the vegetables and carefully transfer the lengua to a cutting board. When cool enough to handle but still very warm, peel the skin (you might have to use a knife in some areas) and discard. Cut the lengua into ¾-in [2-cm] slices (cut at a slight angle following the shape of the tongue). If not using right away, store, tightly covered in plastic wrap, in the refrigerator for up to 2 days.

When ready to serve, heat the oven to 350°F [180°C].

Mix the flour and 1 tsp of salt with a fork or whisk in a medium bowl. Put the eggs in another bowl, and the panko in a third bowl. Using one hand, dredge a slice of lengua in the flour to lightly coat it. With the other hand, gently dip it into the beaten egg, shaking off any excess, then pass the lengua through the panko so that it is evenly coated. Set aside on a plate. Repeat with the remaining lengua slices.

Line a plate with paper towels. Heat the oil in a large cast-iron frying pan over medium-high heat until hot and shimmering. Carefully put the lengua slices in the pan and fry until the bottom of each slice is golden brown, 1 to 2 minutes. Flip them over and fry until golden brown on the second side, about 1 minute longer.

Transfer the pan to the oven and heat until the lengua is warmed through, about 8 minutes. Transfer the lengua to the paper towel–lined plate and set aside.

cont'd

Wipe the pan clean with a paper towel. Return the pan to medium heat. Add the butter and cook, whisking frequently, until the milk solids begin to brown, about 2 minutes. It will first foam a little, then subside, and lightly browned specks will form at the bottom of the pan (there should be a nutty aroma, but watch that it doesn't burn). Add the lemon juice, capers, and tomatoes and cook, stirring occasionally, until the tomatoes begin to release their juices, about 1 minute. Stir in the fenugreek, urfa biber (if using), and mint and remove the pan from the heat.

Transfer the lengua to a platter. Pour the tomato-caper mixture over the top and serve immediately.

Bäco flatbread

At Bäco Mercat, "bread" means flatbread, the foundation for the Bäco sandwiches that the restaurant is named for. The kitchen makes up to several hundred flatbreads a day, a ritual of mixing, proofing, rolling, and griddling fresh dough. The process of making them at home is the same, with all of the ingredients easily mixed by hand in one bowl. Hot off the stove, the oval breads are warm and soft and blistered with browned, bubbled spots—these spots are the marks of their deliciousness.

The breads, for the most part, are dedicated to Bäco sandwiches. The Bäco has been described in a lot of ways—"a gyro-taco-pizza hybrid" or a "grand buffet in a sandwich," for example—with ingredients that bring together the flavors of the Eastern Mediterranean, Spain, North Africa, Mexico, and Asia. It's also particular to Los Angeles. It's a street food–inspired dish that I first made as a staff meal years ago. I piled flatbread with crisped pork belly and "carnitas" made from beef shoulder, sauced it with romesco and salbitxada, added greens and pickles, and the result ended up inspiring a restaurant.

The recipe for the flatbread has evolved over the years and includes ghee and yogurt for rich and tender breads, like Indian naan. As the bread cooks, its surface browns and bubbles and slightly crisps, and the interior crumb begins to steam and rise and puff. It's buttery and brown-splotched and pliable enough to wrap around fillings.

Serve a stack of flatbread at the dinner table, to use for scooping creamy yogurt or dips, sopping up the juices of rosy, meaty roasts, or as an accompaniment for mezze. In the mornings, I like them wrapped around soft-scrambled eggs and chorizo. At Bäco Mercat, they're also served smeared with chimichurri, folded, and cut into pieces for dipping in a mixture of yogurt, fava hummus, and eggplant purée with garlic, sumac, and za'atar (page 226).

Or, of course, you can use them for sandwiches.

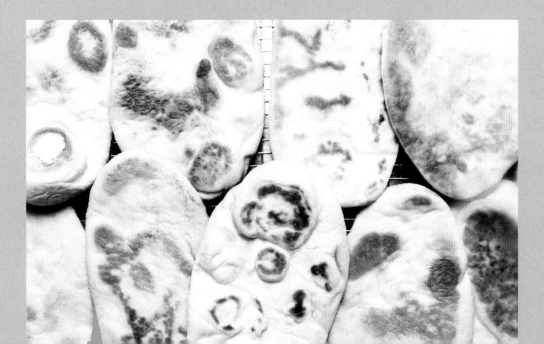

Bäco bread

1½ tsp active dry yeast
1½ tsp sugar
1 cup [240 ml] warm water
3⅔ cups [440 g] flour, plus more for dusting
2 tsp salt
6 Tbsp [80 g] ghee (page 86), at room temperature
3 Tbsp plain yogurt
Avocado or olive oil for cooking

Whisk together the yeast, sugar, and warm water in a small bowl. Set aside until foamy, about 10 minutes.

Whisk together the flour and salt in a large bowl. Add the ghee, yogurt, and yeast mixture and mix with a wooden spoon or by hand until thoroughly combined. Turn the dough out onto a floured work surface and knead until smooth and supple, about 10 minutes.

Transfer the dough to an oiled bowl, cover with plastic wrap, and set aside until nearly doubled in volume, about 1½ hours.

Punch down the dough, turn it out onto a lightly floured work surface, and knead it again for a few minutes. Cut the dough into 10 pieces and roll each piece into a ball. With a rolling pin, roll out each ball into an 8-by-4-in [20-by-10-cm] oval, dusting with flour as needed.

Heat the oven to 300°F [150°C]. Heat 1 Tbsp oil in a large heavy-bottomed frying pan over medium-high heat until hot and shimmering. Place one piece of dough in the pan, adjusting the heat as needed so that the bread is browned on the bottom and the top starts to bubble and puff, about 1 minute. Flip the bread and cook until the second side is browned, about 1 minute longer. The breads should be spotted with well-browned areas and still pliable.

Transfer to a baking sheet and keep warm in the oven while you cook the remaining breads, adding more oil to the pan as needed. Serve warm.

The beauty of the Bäco bread is that it's a vessel for so many fillings, with the bread folded around all the things I like to cook and all the flavors that I love—grilled meats, vegetables, fritters, creamy sauces, vinegary sauces, crunchy slaws, fresh herbs.

I tend to use more than one sauce. The original Bäco sandwich, for example, is sauced with smoked paprika aioli, chimichurri, salbitxada, and romesco.

Throughout this book there are recipes that can be used as fillings, sauces, and garnishes for the flatbreads:

PANKO-CRUSTED SHRIMP WITH CHIVES AND MEXICAN SRIRACHA (PAGE 148)

CHICKEN ESCABECHE WITH MINT (PAGE 252)

CUMIN-SPICED BEEF AND LAMB PATTIES WITH PINE NUTS AND RAISINS (PAGE 260)

BULGUR PANCAKES WITH GRAPE LEAVES, RAISINS, AND GOAT CHEESE (PAGE 193)

POTATO CROQUETTES (PAGE 151)

BAHARAT-SPICED PORCHETTA (PAGE 258)

SICHUAN PEPPER LAMB TOP ROUND WITH ENGLISH PEA AND PARSLEY SALAD (PAGE 246)

SKIRT STEAK WITH HORSERADISH YOGURT AND BEETS BI TAHINA (PAGE 249)

WHOLE ROASTED ORANGE- AND SOY-GLAZED DUCK (PAGE 267)

COFFEE-RUBBED PRIME RIB WITH MINT AND ROSE PICKLED RED ONIONS (PAGE 270)

LENGUA "SCHNITZEL" WITH BROWN BUTTER, CAPERS, AND CHERRY TOMATOES (PAGE 172)

CABBAGE SLAW WITH CRÈME FRAÎCHE, MITSUBA, AND KOCHKOCHA (PAGE 102)

ADJIKA VINAIGRETTE (PAGE 64)

CHIMICHURRI (PAGE 84)

POBLANO-FETA DIP (PAGE 79)

MORTAR-AND-PESTLE HARISSA (PAGE 62)

KOCHKOCHA (PAGE 82)

MINT AND ROSE PICKLED RED ONIONS (PAGE 22)

MORTAR-AND-PESTLE ROMESCO (PAGE 60)

SALBITXADA (PAGE 63)

MINT AND FINES HERBES SALSA VERDE (PAGE 70)

AONORI MASCARPONE BUTTER (PAGE 88)

CHERMOU-LATA BUTTER (PAGE 69)

For sandwiches, add fresh greens such as arugula, watercress, endive, Little Gem lettuce, or a mix, along with lots of herbs such as parsley, chives, chervil, cilantro, basil, and mint.

I remember the way the air smelled as soon as the rain hit the ground in San Antonio: fresh and sweet and of the earth. It has always been one of my favorite sensory memories, and it's at least partly why I am big on a lot of vegetables with of-the-fields flavor: beets, mushrooms, eggplants, potatoes, legumes, grains, woody herbs, and earthy spices. Beets actually contain geosmin, an organic compound that smells like a plowed field just after a rain.

One of my first kitchen jobs was in a vegetarian restaurant in Austin, where beets might have been revered as much as they must have been at Chez Panisse (even if they mostly ended up in juice). But it wasn't until I was a stage (intern) in the kitchen at Daniel in New York that I actually cooked any beets: borscht, topped with crème fraîche and a demitasse-spoonful of caviar.

That was about as close as I got to the beet-and-fresh-chèvre craze, but I think the combination perseveres because rooty, sweet beets and sharp cheeses are so complementary. Roasted beets tossed in parsley butter and served with a chunk of farmer cheese, feta, blue cheese, or funky boucheron and some crusty, salty bread is as good a meal as any. (I might sprinkle furikake or shichimi togarashi over it, too.)

Earthy vegetables and grains call for sharp flavors: vinegars, citrus, pomegranate molasses, grainy mustard, cheeses, yogurt, capers, red wine, ginger, chiles. I want a matrix of earthy, sharp, and savory flavors with custardy, velvety, or silky textures. Think ginger, lemon, cumin, turmeric, and chiles in matar dal, the Indian dish of creamy split peas or lentils. Or something as simple as Alsatian boiled potatoes with the traditional combination of Munster cheese and cumin.

I'm less a fan of eggplant melted into a ratatouille, the traditional Provençal vegetable stew, than I am of a salad that highlights its distinct texture, with a sharp tang to punch up its mellow flavor. I like the lemon juice, pome-granate molasses, and yogurt in the Levantine eggplant dips baba ghanoush and moutabal.

One of the best flavor combinations I know is savory, nutty brown butter with bright, tart lemon juice, especially as a vinaigrette for tender beans or a sauce for earthy pasta.

Fava bean or English pea hummus I make with lemon juice, lemon zest, and plenty of the salty Italian sheep's milk cheese Pecorino Romano. I'll split open a slow-roasted starchy-velvety sweet potato and fill it with a combination of feta, honey, and mascarpone butter flavored with the ground Japanese seaweed aonori. Not bad for a humble potato.

earthy

sharp

5

velvety

savory

Beets bi tahina

Beet "hummus" is an oxymoron. *Hummus* is the Arabic word for "chickpeas" (the full name for the Middle Eastern hummus we know and love is *hummus bi tahina*, or "chickpeas with tahini"). But this brilliantly colored beet version is hummus in spirit, a creamy, textured dip for smearing onto vegetables or flatbreads. And it otherwise has all of the same ingredients as chickpea hummus—sesame paste, lemon juice, and garlic. I like this earthy-but-bright beet "hummus" as a dip, swirled with a little yogurt, for crudités, or spread on toast with ricotta or fresh goat cheese or farmer cheese. I also use it as a condiment to serve alongside a roast or steak (page 249).

NOTE: I use Japanese sesame paste, labeled atari goma, which can be found at Japanese markets and online. It can be substituted with high-quality unsalted tahini.

MAKES ABOUT 1 CUP [220 G]

2 beets, about 9 oz [250 g] total
½ Tbsp olive oil
Salt
Fresh black pepper
2 Tbsp water
1 sprig thyme
1 small garlic clove, peeled
2 to 3 Tbsp sesame paste
2 Tbsp white sesame seeds
Juice of ½ lemon

Heat the oven to 400°F [200°C].

Place the beets in the center of a large piece of aluminum foil. Coat the beets with the olive oil and season with a pinch of salt and a few grinds of black pepper. Add the water and thyme and fold the foil into a sealed packet. Put the foil packet on a baking sheet and roast the beets until tender, 45 to 60 minutes. Remove from the oven and set aside. When cool enough to handle, peel the beets and set aside to cool completely. Discard the thyme.

Put the beets, garlic, sesame paste, sesame seeds, lemon juice, and ½ tsp salt in a food processor and pulse to a coarse purée. Serve immediately or store, covered, in the refrigerator for up to 2 days.

English pea and dill "hummus"

Another "hummus." In addition to using English peas instead of chickpeas, this recipe includes dill and Parmigiano-Reggiano along with the traditional sesame paste, garlic, and lemon juice. It is springlike and fresh, and like the beets bi tahina (page 182), has its own vibrant color. Use it anywhere you might use chickpea hummus.

NOTE: I use Japanese sesame paste, labeled atari goma, which can be found at Japanese markets and online. It can be substituted with high-quality unsalted tahini.

MAKES ABOUT 1½ CUPS [330 G]

2 cups [320 g] shelled English peas
1 small garlic clove, peeled
¼ cup [60 ml] olive oil
3 Tbsp grated Parmigiano-Reggiano
2 Tbsp sesame paste
2 Tbsp dill fronds
1 tsp salt
1 tsp fresh lemon juice

Prepare an ice bath by filling a large bowl with ice water. Set aside.

Bring a medium saucepan of salted water to boil over high heat. Add the peas and blanch until just tender, about 3 minutes. Drain the peas and transfer them to the ice bath to cool. Drain again and set aside.

Put the garlic and olive oil in a food processor and process until blended. Add the blanched peas, Parmigiano, and sesame paste and pulse to a coarse purée. Add the dill, salt, and lemon juice and pulse until incorporated. Serve immediately or store in a covered container in the refrigerator for up to 2 days.

Fuyu persimmon salad with grapes, red walnuts, and sherry vinegar

Persimmons are a fruit revered in California, where they have been cultivated since the 1800s. Their season reaches its peak in November, and the arrival of persimmons each year in Los Angeles practically means fall. Fuyu and Hachiya are the most common varieties here. Fuyu has a flatter top and is best when firm, and Hachiya is shaped like an acorn and eaten when ripe and soft. For salads, I like crunchy Fuyu persimmons, dressed lightly and mixed with pomegranate seeds, late-harvest grapes, and a mix of herbs. Also in season in the fall are California red walnuts, a cross between red-skinned Persian and creamier English walnuts. These are big, oily, and sweet and pair well with persimmons. For a richer salad, add a few slices of nutty, custardy Hass avocado; the sherry vinegar helps cut through its richness.

NOTE: In the transition between summer and fall, persimmons and grapes are available at farmers' markets. I like Moon Drop grapes for the elongated, oval shape; you might also find seedless Thompson, Kyoho, and Summer Royal.

SERVES 4

2 firm Fuyu persimmons
½ cup [70 g] grapes, halved lengthwise
¼ cup [40 g] pomegranate seeds
¼ cup [30 g] walnuts, preferably red walnuts
1 Tbsp chopped fresh chives
2 tsp finely chopped shallot
Fresh black pepper
1 Tbsp sherry vinegar
Pinch of salt
2 Tbsp extra-virgin olive oil
1 Tbsp chopped fresh mint
1 Tbsp chopped fresh parsley
1 Tbsp chopped dill fronds
½ ripe Hass avocado, peeled, pitted, and cut into fat slices or cubed (optional)

Quarter the persimmons and put in a large bowl. Add the grapes, pomegranate seeds, walnuts, chives, shallot, and a few grinds of black pepper. Set aside.

Whisk together the sherry vinegar and salt in a small bowl. Add the olive oil and whisk to combine. Toss the persimmon mixture with the vinaigrette. Add the mint, parsley, and dill and toss again. Gently fold in the avocado (if using). Serve immediately.

Sweet potatoes with aonori mascarpone butter, feta, and honey

These remind me of one of my mom's favorite things to eat: roasted sweet potato slathered with butter and sprinkled with salt. The sweet potatoes here are dressed with a little bit of honey, crumbled feta, and homemade butter that's been gently folded with mascarpone and toasty ground seaweed, so that they're savory, sweet, creamy, sticky, briny, and tangy all at once. Depending on the variety of sweet potato, the interior is steamy and custardy or firm and starchy. Sometimes they're garnet yams with red-purple skin and a supermoist interior, or malty-sweet Covingtons, or Korean purples, which are actually white-fleshed and have a chestnut-like flavor. Lately I've leaned toward Okinawan or Stokes sweet potatoes for their color—purple or magenta on the inside, respectively—and because they hold their shape so well.

SERVES 6

3 medium sweet potatoes or yams, preferably purple, scrubbed but not peeled

1 Tbsp olive oil

Salt

6 Tbsp [75 g] aonori mascarpone butter (page 88)

¼ cup [75 g] honey

¾ cup [105 g] crumbled feta

1 Tbsp finely chopped fresh chives

Heat the oven to 400°F [200°C] with a rack set at the second-lowest position.

Rub the sweet potatoes with the olive oil. Prick the potatoes all over with a fork and sprinkle with salt. Wrap each of the potatoes in aluminum foil and seal tightly. Place them directly on the oven rack and bake until quite soft and a knife easily glides through when a potato is pierced. Check after about 1 hour, and if not soft, return to the oven and check again in 10 minutes. Remove from the oven and carefully unwrap the potatoes.

While the potatoes are still hot, carefully cut each potato in half lengthwise. Season the cut side of each half with a pinch of salt. Top with 1 Tbsp of aonori mascarpone butter and a drizzle of honey. Sprinkle the feta and chives over the top, dividing them evenly among the potatoes. Serve immediately.

Rutabaga and pancetta with lemon, anchovy, and capers

Rutabagas are one of my favorite winter vegetables. A cross between a cabbage and a turnip, they taste like a rich, less starchy potato when cooked. I like their like-a-carrot-but-less-sweet earthiness with meaty pancetta (Italian cured but not smoked pork belly) or bacon and all the flavors of a bright-sharp salsa verde, including tangy Dijon mustard, briny-rich anchovies, tart lemon, and aromatic garlic. The pancetta is just crisped but still tender, and the rutabaga has a lush quality. Use an extra just-picked herb or sliced scallions as garnish for an element of freshness. This might be considered a side dish, but I eat it with a salad of greens and call it dinner.

NOTE: White anchovies, also known as boquerones, are anchovies cured in vinegar (or vinegar and olive oil), causing the fillets to turn white. They're available at select supermarkets and online.

SERVES 4 TO 6

DRESSING

½ cup [7 g] fresh parsley leaves, chopped

2 white anchovy fillets, rinsed and finely chopped

¼ cup [60 ml] olive oil

Grated zest of 1 lemon

Juice of ½ lemon

1 Tbsp capers, chopped

¼ tsp chopped garlic

1 tsp Dijon mustard

Pinch of red pepper flakes

Pinch of salt

3 rutabagas, about 3 lb [1.4 kg], trimmed and peeled

4 oz [115 g] pancetta or slab bacon (½ in [12 mm] thick, if sliced)

2 Tbsp avocado or olive oil

1 Tbsp chopped garlic

¼ tsp salt

Juice of ½ lemon

2 scallions, green part only, cut into very thin slices on the bias

cont'd

MAKE THE DRESSING: Whisk together the parsley, anchovies, olive oil, lemon zest, lemon juice, capers, garlic, mustard, red pepper flakes, and salt in a bowl. Set aside.

Bring a large pot of salted water to a boil over high heat.

Cut each rutabaga in half and cut each half into ¾-in [2-cm] slices. Lay each slice flat and cut into large ¾-in- [2-cm-] wide batons. Add the rutabaga to the boiling water and cook until al dente, about 3 minutes. Drain and set aside.

Cut the pancetta into lardons that are ½ in by ½ in by 1½ in [12 mm by 12 mm by 4 cm]. Line a plate with paper towels. Heat a small frying pan over medium heat, add the pancetta, and sauté until the fat renders, 2 to 3 minutes. Remove from the heat. Transfer to the paper towel–lined plate to drain. Set aside.

Heat the oil in a large sauté pan over medium-high heat until hot and shimmering. Add the rutabagas and sauté until tender and the edges are well browned, about 5 minutes. Add the pancetta, garlic, and salt and cook for 1 minute longer. Remove from the heat. Add the lemon juice and toss with all but a couple of tablespoons of the dressing.

Transfer to a platter. Drizzle the remaining dressing and scatter the scallions over the top. Serve immediately.

Bulgur pancakes with grape leaves, raisins, and goat cheese

These are what I also call inside-out stuffed grape leaves. You don't have to carefully wrap and fold each grape leaf, as you would with dolma. Instead, the grape leaves are sliced and used to season the bulgur, along with za'atar and fresh herbs. Serve with roasts or whole fish, or use these for a vegetarian sandwich, a different take on falafel.

SERVES 8

2 cups [480 ml] water
Salt
1 cup [200 g] bulgur
¼ cup [50 g] golden raisins
¼ cup [30 g] za'atar
6 fresh mint leaves, chopped
¼ cup [4 g] fresh parsley leaves, chopped
10 brined grape leaves, cut into thin slices
⅓ cup [40 g] flour
½ cup [120 ml] fresh orange juice
½ tsp grated lemon zest
1 tsp fresh lemon juice
2 eggs
½ cup [55 g] crumbled fresh goat cheese
Avocado or olive oil for cooking

Bring the water and 1 tsp salt to a boil in a saucepan over high heat. Put the bulgur in a large heatproof bowl and pour the boiling water over. Cover tightly with plastic wrap and let stand until tender, about 10 minutes. If there's excess water, drain and refrigerate, covered, for 20 minutes and up to overnight.

Add the raisins, za'atar, mint, parsley, grape leaves, flour, orange juice, lemon zest, lemon juice, eggs, and ½ tsp salt and stir until combined. Add the goat cheese and very gently stir it in using your hands.

Heat the oven to 200°F [95°C]. Heat 1 Tbsp oil in a frying pan over medium-high heat until hot and shimmering. Spoon the batter into the pan, forming pancakes that are no more than 4 in [10 cm] across. Cook the pancakes until the bottoms are browned, about 2 minutes. Flip and cook the second side until browned, about 2 minutes longer. Transfer to a plate and keep warm in the oven. Repeat, adding oil as needed, until you've cooked all of the batter. Serve immediately.

Eggplant with avocado, Persian cucumbers, herbs, and cipollini-buttermilk dressing

This vegetable salad mixes lots of flavors, textures, and temperatures. There is both raw and cooked, rich and refreshing, creamy and crunchy, bright and earthy. The combination of caramelized eggplant and creamy avocado is rich, but it's balanced by the crunch of juicy cucumbers, fresh herbs, and several elements that bring acidity and brightness. These are lemon zest, vinegar, and tart buttermilk. I prefer to use small eggplants so that they're easy to cook through; make sure that they're not sliced too thickly. When seared, they should get good color (really browned), with charred edges. Putting the egg-plants in the oven for a few minutes gives them a tender interior.

NOTE: You can substitute walnut vinaigrette (page 107) for the cipollini-buttermilk dressing.

SERVES 4

3 to 5 Japanese eggplants, about 14 oz [400 g] total

¼ cup [60 ml] avocado or olive oil

¾ tsp salt

2 cucumbers, preferably Persian, about 4 oz [115 g] total

¼ cup [4 g] fresh parsley leaves

3 Tbsp finely chopped shallot

3 Tbsp chopped fresh chives

3 Tbsp grated lemon zest

3 Tbsp "broken" cipollini-buttermilk dressing (page 74)

Fresh black pepper

1 ripe avocado peeled, pitted, and cut into large dice

½ lemon

Heat the oven to 375°F [190°C].

Cut the eggplants in half lengthwise, then cut them into ¼-in [6-mm] slices on the bias.

Heat the oil in a large cast-iron frying pan over high heat until hot and shimmering. Carefully add the eggplant slices to the frying pan, spreading them as evenly as possible. Sprinkle the eggplant with ½ tsp of the salt and sear until the bottoms are caramelized and golden brown, about 1½ minutes. Working quickly so that the eggplant doesn't burn, flip the slices using a fork or offset spatula. Sear until caramel-ized and golden brown on the second side, about 1½ minutes longer.

Remove from the heat and transfer the pan to the oven. Roast the eggplant until cooked through and soft, 3 to 5 minutes. Remove from the oven and transfer to a large bowl. Set aside.

Cut the cucumbers in half lengthwise, then cut them into ¼-in [6-mm] slices on the bias. Add the cucumbers and parsley to the bowl with the eggplant. Set aside.

Mix the shallot, chives, and lemon zest in a small bowl. Add half of the shallot-chive-zest mixture, the cipollini-buttermilk dressing, and several grinds of black pepper to the eggplant and cucumbers. Gently fold in the avocado and set aside.

Squeeze the juice from the lemon over the top and sprinkle with the remaining ¼ tsp salt and the remaining shallot-chive-zest mix. Serve immediately.

Berberé chicken and creamy Pecorino rice

The spices of berberé (more than a dozen of them) along with aromatic garlic and shallots infuse this dish of crisp chicken and creamy, earthy rice with a lot of rich flavors. The Ethiopian spice mixture is one of my favorite rubs for meat—chicken, pork roasts, steaks, lamb. Here it's used for the chicken, and it spices the rice, too. Added to the rice are cream, Pecorino, lemon, fresh ginger, and herbs, including a handful of funky, savory curry leaves. I use a Japanese rice called Satsuki grown in Uruguay by a friend and former Los Angeles sushi chef. Use any short-grain rice, but I like the Koshihikari variety.

NOTE: Curry leaves are available at some Indian markets, farmers' markets, and online. Curry and bay leaves aren't exactly interchangeable, flavor- or intensity-wise, but bay leaf works here as a good substitute. Use 1 fresh bay leaf (its aromatic menthol flavor is strong) in place of the curry leaves.

SERVES 4

About 3 lb [1.4 kg] whole chicken legs (thighs separated)

1½ Tbsp berberé (page 36)

Salt

3 Tbsp avocado or olive oil

5 shallots, cut into thin slices

1 garlic clove, cut into thin slices, plus ½ garlic clove, grated with a zester

1⅓ cups [265 g] short-grain rice

1⅓ cups [320 ml] dry white wine

2 cups [480 ml] chicken broth or water

3 Tbsp grated Pecorino cheese

20 fresh curry leaves

4 slices lemon, with the rind, plus ½ lemon

1 oz [30 g] fresh ginger, peeled and cut into slices

1 cup [240 ml] heavy cream

Fresh black pepper

½ cup [7 g] fresh parsley leaves

½ cup [8 g] fresh mint leaves

1 scallion, green part only, cut into thin slices on the bias

Place the chicken in a large bowl and add 1 Tbsp of the berberé and 1 tsp salt. Toss until the chicken is seasoned on all sides with the spice mixture.

cont'd

Heat the oil in a wide, high-sided frying or sauté pan over high heat until hot and shimmering. Add the chicken to the pan, skin side down, and sear until very crispy and well browned, about 5 minutes. Flip the pieces of chicken and sear on the second side for 1 minute longer. Carefully remove the chicken from the pan, transfer to a plate, and set aside.

Heat the pan over medium-high heat, add the shallots and sliced garlic, and sweat, stirring occasionally, until they are aromatic and begin to lose their moisture but do not color, 2 to 3 minutes. Add the rice, ½ tsp salt, and the remaining ½ Tbsp berberé and toast the rice, stirring to coat the rice with the spices, for 1 minute.

Add the wine and cook until the rice has absorbed the liquid (it should be fairly dry), 2 to 3 minutes. Add the broth, sprinkle with 1 Tbsp of the Pecorino, and add the curry leaves, lemon slices, and ginger. Place the chicken over the rice mixture, bring it to a simmer, and cover. Cook until the rice is just tender, about 17 minutes. The internal temperature of the chicken should reach at least 165°F [75°C] by the time the rice is cooked.

Meanwhile, heat the cream, grated garlic, 4 grinds of black pepper, a pinch of salt, and the remaining 2 Tbsp Pecorino in a small saucepan over medium-high heat, whisking frequently, until the mixture reaches a boil. Lower the heat and simmer for 1 minute, continuing to whisk, then immediately remove from the heat. Set aside.

When the rice has finished cooking, remove from the heat and pour the warm cream mixture over the rice. Squeeze the juice from the ½ lemon over the rice and sprinkle with the parsley, mint, and scallion. Serve immediately.

Hand-torn pasta

The legendary Alice Waters came in one night when I was the chef at a down-town L.A. restaurant called Lazy Ox, and she ordered hand-torn pasta with fried egg and brown butter. I was so nervous I made it twice before I would serve it to her, and then watched her from the kitchen while she ate it. The server came back a little later and told me she hadn't even finished it yet but wanted a second bowl. And when I finally got the courage to go to her table to meet her, she grabbed my hand and said the pasta was so delicious that she had to have two orders. Now this is my go-to pasta dough recipe. I let this pasta dry out a little after rolling so that it's easier to tear but not so much that it breaks. When cooked, it's delicate, silky, and supple.

NOTE: The quality of the eggs makes a difference in the taste and appearance of the pasta; it's worth looking for organic eggs from pasture-raised chickens.

MAKES ABOUT 1⅓ LB [605 G] PASTA, ENOUGH FOR 4 TO 6 SERVINGS

3 cups [360 g] flour, plus more for dusting
1½ tsp salt
1 egg plus 4 egg yolks
½ cup [120 ml] cold water

Put the flour and salt in the bowl of a stand mixer fitted with the paddle attachment and mix on low speed until well combined. Add the egg, egg yolks, and cold water and mix on low speed until the dough is stiff and smooth, about 10 minutes.

Remove the dough from the mixer, transfer it to a floured work sur-face, and knead it for 2 minutes. Place the dough in a bowl, cover it with a kitchen towel or plastic wrap, and let rest in the refrigerator for 20 minutes.

Cut the dough into quarters and roll into logs. Work with one log at a time; cover the remaining dough with plastic wrap and set aside.

Slightly flatten the unwrapped log of dough into an oval shape. Roll the dough with a rolling pin until it's about ¼ in [6 mm] thick and 3 in [7.5 cm] wide; make sure it is rolled thin enough to go through the rollers of a pasta machine without bunching up. Gently place the dough through the rollers of a pasta machine or the mixer's pasta attachment, starting on the widest setting. Send it through the first setting again, then lightly dust the rolled pasta with flour.

cont'd

Reduce the setting of the rollers by one notch and place the dough through the rollers again. Gently support the exiting dough with the back of your hand and lightly dust with flour. Continue to move the dough through the rollers, dusting with flour after each turn; reduce the thickness setting by one notch each time until you reach the second-to-thinnest setting (usually marked number 6 on a pasta machine).

Place the sheet of dough on a lightly floured surface or a pasta rack until dry (it shouldn't be brittle but just dry enough to tear into sheets), about 15 minutes.

Roll each log of the remaining dough the same way.

When dried, tear the pasta crosswise into roughly equal squares. I like to use a bench scraper to help tear the sheets of pasta. They should be about 5 by 5 in [12 by 12 cm], but they don't need to be—and shouldn't be—perfect. If not using right away, store the dough in a paper bag in the refrigerator for up to 3 days.

VARIATION

Pappardelle: To make pappardelle, mix and roll the dough in the same way, but stop at a thicker setting—two or three notches before the thinnest setting (usually marked number 5 on a pasta machine). As soon as you've finished rolling the dough, make sure it's well floured and fold the dough from each end until they meet in the middle. Fold end to end again. Cut the dough into 1-in- [2.5-cm-] wide strips. Place them on a rimmed baking sheet and cover with a kitchen towel until ready to cook. If not using right away, make sure the pasta is well floured, then form several strands at a time into nests and put into sealed plastic bags. Refrigerate for up to 2 days or freeze for up to 2 months.

Hand-torn pasta with yuzu, dashi, and brown butter

I especially love the combination of tart citrus and nutty, rich brown butter. The two together are an epiphany. Yuzu is tart like grapefruit but not bitter and has notes of mandarin orange. It's just as delicious as lemon with the toasty, caramely milk solids of brown butter. The finished dish looks so simple but has so much flavor.

NOTE: See the note on page 122 about bottled shiro dashi, which can be substituted for the dashi concentrate. High-quality bottled yuzu juice is available at Japanese markets and online.

SERVES 4

2½ Tbsp [35 g] butter

1 Tbsp yuzu juice, or to taste

1 Tbsp dashi concentrate (page 76), or to taste

1 lb [455 g] hand-torn pasta (page 201)

3 Tbsp grated Parmigiano-Reggiano

1 Tbsp chopped fresh parsley

1 Tbsp chopped fresh chervil

1 Tbsp chopped fresh chives

Fresh black pepper

Olive oil (optional)

Melt the butter in a frying pan over medium-high heat and continue to cook, whisking frequently, until the milk solids begin to brown, 1 to 2 minutes. It will first foam a little, then subside, and lightly browned specks will form at the bottom of the pan (there should be a nutty aroma, but watch that it doesn't burn). Stir in the yuzu juice and dashi concentrate and remove from the heat. Set aside.

Bring a large pot of salted water to a rolling boil over high heat. Add the hand-torn pasta, one or two pieces at a time, to the boiling water; don't drop all of the pieces in at once or they will stick together. Boil until al dente, 1 to 2 minutes.

cont'd

Stir gently with a wooden spoon and, using a skimmer, remove a few pieces at a time from the water; be sure to drain thoroughly. The pasta is thin and delicate, so it's best to work quickly. Transfer the pasta to a large bowl. Pour the brown butter mixture over the pasta and gently stir to evenly coat. Taste and add more yuzu or dashi as desired. Sprinkle with the Parmigiano-Reggiano, parsley, chervil, and chives, and a few grinds of black pepper. Add a little of the hot pasta water and/or olive oil if it starts to stick.

Divide the pasta among four bowls and serve immediately.

Pork belly with sujuk spices and hand-torn pasta

One of my favorite pasta sauces is something like a cross between the Armenian sausage sujuk and an Italian pork ragù. The flavors are inspired by sujuk's bold spicing (here it's cumin, fenugreek, Aleppo pepper, and allspice), brightened with tomatoes and fresh herbs. I like this combination a lot—it's heady and bright and unusual and comforting all at once. Sometimes I make spinach cavatelli and sometimes hand-torn pasta (page 201) for this dish, enriched with a knob of butter and a hit of Pecorino at the end.

NOTE: This recipe calls for a meat grinder or stand mixer's meat grinding attachment; the meat and any grinding equipment—such as the grinding tray, auger, blade, and plates—should be cold (put them in the freezer for 45 to 60 minutes). Use a grinding plate with ⅜-in [1-cm] holes. Alternatively, if you don't have a meat grinder, ask your butcher to coarsely grind the pork belly.

SERVES 4

1 tsp whole cloves

1½ tsp cumin seeds

1 tsp whole allspice

1 tsp dried fenugreek leaves

1 tsp ground cinnamon

1 tsp ground ginger

1 tsp freshly grated nutmeg

1 tsp Aleppo pepper

2 tsp freshly ground black pepper

2 lb [910 g] skinless pork belly

2 Tbsp avocado or olive oil

6 whole peeled canned tomatoes, coarsely chopped, with juices

Salt

1 recipe hand-torn pasta (page 201)

2 Tbsp butter, cut into pieces

¼ cup [4 g] dill fronds, chopped

¼ cup [3 g] fresh tarragon leaves, chopped

3 Tbsp chopped fresh chives

3 Tbsp grated Pecorino cheese

cont'd

Toast the cloves, cumin, and allspice in a small, dry frying pan over medium heat, stirring occasionally, until fragrant, 2 to 3 minutes. Grind the seeds and fenugreek leaves to a fine powder in a spice grinder or with a mortar and pestle.

Transfer the spice mixture to a large bowl. Stir in the cinnamon, ginger, nutmeg, Aleppo pepper, and black pepper. Set aside.

Cut the pork belly crosswise into 1½-in [4-cm] pieces and add to the bowl of spices. Season the meat by rubbing it with the spices.

Grind the meat using a meat grinder or a stand mixer's meat grinder attachment. Fit the grinder or mixer with a plate with ⅜-in (1-cm) holes and grind the cubed pork belly.

If using already ground meat, add the meat to the bowl of spices and mix gently but thoroughly.

Heat 1 Tbsp of the oil in a large frying pan over medium heat until hot and shimmering. Add the spiced pork belly and cook, stirring occasionally, until it starts to brown and the fat is rendered, about 7 minutes. Carefully pour off the excess fat and discard.

Add the tomatoes with their juice and 1 tsp salt and cook over medium-high heat until the tomatoes begin to break down, about 3 minutes. Return the pork belly to the pan and cover. Turn the heat to low and keep warm.

Bring a large pot of salted water to a rolling boil over high heat. Add the hand-torn pasta, one or two pieces at a time, to the boiling water; don't drop all of the pieces in at once or they will stick together. Boil until al dente, 1 to 2 minutes.

Stir gently with a wooden spoon and, using a skimmer, remove a few pieces at a time from the water; be sure to drain thoroughly. The pasta is thin and delicate, so it's best to work quickly. Transfer the pasta to a large bowl. Add the butter, remaining 1 Tbsp oil, dill, tarragon, chives, and Pecorino; gently toss to coat the pasta.

Divide the pasta among four pasta bowls or four plates. Remove the pork belly and tomato sauce from the heat. Top the pasta with the desired amount of pork belly and sauce. Serve immediately.

In the French restaurant kitchens of New York, I remember making pommes purée the way a lot of chefs did—in the style of Joël Robuchon. I peeled fingerling potatoes one by one while they were still hot enough to burn my fingertips (they had to be hot or the purée would turn out gummy); riced them; whisked in at least half their weight in butter, plus steamed milk; then passed them through a tamis (a drum-shaped fine strainer), twice. Those potatoes were pure velvet.

But a lot of the time creamy is easy. It can be the result of a simple preparation. The bowlfuls of warm Cream of Wheat that I ate when I was a kid back then seemed like as much a luxury as those ultra-creamy potatoes. I started serving Cream of Wheat on tasting menus when once in the middle of service I ran out of polenta, sent a cook to the store, and he came back with the farina in the red box instead. I made do. I stirred in milk, butter, and a handful of grated Parmigiano-Reggiano, and it went with red wine–lacquered braised beef. Cream of Wheat saved the day, and I still serve farina this way.

In fact, I like all kinds of creamy porridge: steel-cut oats with cream, hazelnuts, and sautéed peaches; grits with tahini and oven-roasted baby tomatoes; or short-grain rice and Pecorino cream topped with geoduck, uni, and seared scallops. Creamy soups and stews, too. Creamy dips, of course. Custards savory or sweet. Or just the right amount of soft cheese or cool yogurt to accent fresh pasta, tender beans, or baba ghanoush. A little creamy goes a long way.

It's a texture that calls for layering flavors, whether spicy and sweet, herbal and citrusy, or nutty and floral, to name a few. Freshly made pudding-like tofu with sesame, ginger, and honey. Pistachio panna cotta with crunchy spring vegetables. Cheesy polenta with crème fraîche and arbol-guajillo furikake.

Some of the best creamy dishes balance richness with other textures. And it is especially good with crunchy: nuts, seeds, dukkah (nuts and seeds), toasted croutons or grains, and raw vegetables.

Among my favorite soups is one made with roasted poblano chiles and cream, topped with crispy pancetta and crunchy pickled grapes. The grapes are unexpected in a savory, creamy soup, but they add just the right tartness to match poblanos' subtle heat and floral notes. And their particular juicy snap is what makes the dish.

creamy

nutty

crunchy

floral

Barley porridge with ginger and sautéed oranges

Nutty, chewy barley makes a delicious porridge, especially with heavy cream. I like its golden color and sturdy texture. Hulled barley is a whole grain. Only its outer hull is removed (because it isn't edible), so it still retains its bran and endosperm. I prefer barley with a little bit of a bite, even in porridge. I start checking for doneness after the barley has been on the stove for just about 25 minutes. By cooking it with coins of fresh ginger and kaffir lime leaves, the porridge is infused with floral, spicy, citrusy flavors. Caramelized oranges and dukkah make it sweet, warm, spicy, and crunchy.

NOTE: Kaffir lime leaves are available at some Asian markets and online. Japanese black sugar is unrefined cane sugar, which contains molasses and is sold in blocks or chunks. Traditional in Okinawa, it's smoky, malty, and a little salty. Available at Japanese markets or online.

SERVES 6

4 cups [950 ml] water

2 cups [340 g] hulled barley

1 tsp salt

3 kaffir lime leaves

1 oz [30 g] fresh ginger, peeled and cut into slices

1½ oz [40 g] grated Japanese black sugar or 3 Tbsp dark brown sugar

1 cup [240 ml] heavy cream, plus more for garnish

2 oranges or 4 blood oranges

1½ tsp granulated sugar

1 Tbsp butter

2 Tbsp cashew and coconut breakfast dukkah (page 52, optional)

Put the water, barley, and salt in a saucepan and bring the water to a boil over high heat. Turn the heat to low and add the kaffir lime leaves, ginger, and black sugar. Simmer the barley, stirring often so that it doesn't stick to the bottom of the pan, until tender but still has a little bit of a bite, about 25 minutes. After 15 minutes of cooking, add the heavy cream. The barley should have texture but shouldn't be al dente. Add a little liquid (water, cream, or milk) if the porridge gets too thick before the barley is cooked; check every 5 minutes until the desired texture is reached.

MEANWHILE, SEGMENT THE ORANGES: Trim a little off the top and bottom of each orange with a sharp knife so that there are two flat ends. Set an orange flat on a cutting surface and cut away the peel and white skin from top to bottom, working your way around the fruit. Remove each citrus segment by cutting between the fruit and the membrane for each section; the wedges should release easily. Transfer to a small bowl and sprinkle with the granulated sugar.

Heat the butter in a frying pan over medium-low heat. When it starts to sizzle, add the orange segments and sear until caramelized and golden brown, 1 to 2 minutes on each side. Remove from the heat and set aside.

Once the barley is tender, remove from the heat and discard the ginger and kaffir lime leaves. Divide the porridge evenly among six bowls. Garnish each bowl with the orange segments. Drizzle with extra cream and sprinkle with a spoonful of dukkah, if desired. Serve immediately.

Chilled buttermilk-cacik soup with dill and walnuts

Cacik—the Turkish yogurt dip—is the base for this creamy, refreshing chilled soup. Just add cold buttermilk and milk, toasted nuts, and dill. Make a double recipe of the cacik for this soup. The soup also gets a bit of a kick from the yuzu kosho (Japanese fermented citrus and chile paste) in this version of cacik. When I can get them, red walnuts are a great pop of color as a garnish; they're available in California in the fall at farmers' markets.

SERVES 4

¼ cup [30 g] walnuts
3½ cups [980 g] cacik (page 92), chilled
1⅓ cups [320 ml] buttermilk
1⅓ cups [320 ml] whole milk
Several dill fronds for garnish

Heat the oven to 350°F [180°C]. Spread the nuts in a single layer in an oven-safe pan and place on a middle rack in the oven. Roast, stirring the nuts once for even cooking, until toasty and fragrant, 10 to 12 minutes. Remove from the oven and cool.

Whisk together the cacik, buttermilk, and milk in a large bowl until well combined. Pour into four bowls. Garnish each bowl with a few sprigs of dill and a few toasted walnuts. Serve immediately.

Poblano soup with pancetta and pickled grapes

This was an on-the-fly soup that I made when a critic walked into a restaurant where I was working at the end of the night and ordered a fourteen-course tasting menu. It is seemingly simple but incorporates a lot of flavors, textures, and temperatures: creamy, crispy, crunchy, spicy, sweet, tart, salty, warm, cold. I usually garnish it with pork belly chicharrón—braised pork belly that has been chilled, sliced, and fried crispy—but pancetta lardons are easy and delicious, too. If you want to make a vegetarian version of this soup, you could garnish it with crispy bread crumbs (page 54) right before serving instead of lardons.

SERVES 4

4 oz [115 g] pancetta or slab bacon (½-in [12-mm] thick, if sliced)

5 poblano chiles

4 cups [950 ml] half-and-half

2 cups [480 ml] heavy cream

1 bunch cilantro, leaves only, chopped

1 Tbsp salt

¼ cup [70 g] pickled rooibos grapes (page 24)

3 Tbsp crème fraîche (page 94)

1 Tbsp chopped fresh chives

Cut the pancetta into pieces that are ½ in by ½ in by 1½ in [12 mm by 12 mm by 4 cm]. Line a plate with paper towels. Heat a small frying pan over medium-high heat, add the pancetta, and sauté until crisp and browned, 4 to 5 minutes. Remove from the heat. Transfer to the paper towel–lined plate to drain. Set aside.

One at a time, char the poblano chiles by placing them directly over the open flame of a gas stove or grill. Turn them with tongs as they are roasting, until the skins of the chiles are charred and blistered all over, 1 to 2 minutes on each side. While they're hot, place them in a large sealable plastic bag to steam for about 10 minutes. Don't let the chiles steam for too long or they'll start to turn brown. Remove the charred skin, rubbing it off gently with the back of a knife. Cut open one side of the chile and remove and discard the stems, seeds, and ribs. Set aside.

Put the half-and-half and heavy cream in a pot, bring to a boil over medium-high heat, then remove from the heat. Add the chiles, cilantro, and salt.

In a blender or with a stick blender, purée until smooth (you may have to do it in batches). Once puréed, pass the mixture through a fine-mesh strainer.

Divide the warm soup among four bowls and top with the pancetta and pickled grapes, dividing them evenly. Add a spoonful of crème fraîche and sprinkle with the chives. Serve immediately.

Roasted golden beets with radishes, cucumbers, hazelnuts, and creamy poblano-feta dressing

Mild yellow beets are a canvas here for a lot of flavors, tethered by the acidity of a simple vinaigrette. There are spicy roasted poblano chiles mixed into a smooth dip; tangy feta cheese (I like French feta here for its creaminess); soft, floral herbs; pickled onion; hazelnuts; and salty dry-cured olives. Add just a little bit of water to the pan with the beets during roasting so that they don't get at all dry.

NOTE: Oil- or dry-cured black olives, such as Beldi, Nyon, or Thassos, are available at select markets and online.

SERVES 4

1¾ lb [795 g] golden or Chioggia beets

1 Tbsp olive oil

¼ tsp kosher salt

Fresh black pepper

2 Tbsp water

Several sprigs thyme

½ cup [70 g] hazelnuts

2 cucumbers, preferably Persian, trimmed

4 oz [115 g] radishes such as French breakfast, Ninja, or Fire and Ice

⅓ cup [55 g] mint and rose pickled red onions (page 22)

¼ cup [40 g] dry- or oil-cured black olives

3 Tbsp dill fronds, torn

3 Tbsp fresh parsley leaves

3 Tbsp fresh tarragon leaves

2 Tbsp extra-virgin olive oil

1 Tbsp sherry vinegar

½ tsp flaky sea salt

¼ cup [60 g] creamy poblano-feta dressing (page 80)

3 oz [85 g] French feta, crumbled

cont'd

Heat the oven to 400°F [200°C].

Place the beets in the center of a large piece of aluminum foil. Coat the beets with the olive oil and season with the salt and a few grinds of black pepper. Add the water and thyme and fold the foil into a sealed packet. Put the foil packet on a baking sheet and roast the beets until tender, 45 to 60 minutes. The tip of a knife should pierce the beets easily. Remove from the oven and set aside. When cool enough to handle, peel the beets and set aside to cool completely. Discard the thyme.

Lower the oven to 350°F [180°C]. Spread the hazelnuts in a single layer on a baking sheet and place on a middle rack in the oven. Roast, stirring the nuts once for even cooking, until toasty and fragrant, 12 to 15 minutes. Remove from the oven. When cool enough to handle, coarsely chop the nuts and set aside.

Cut the cucumbers in half lengthwise, then cut them into ¼-in [6-mm] slices on the bias. Add them to a large bowl. Cut the cooled beets into wedges and add them to the bowl. Quarter the radishes lengthwise and add them to the bowl, along with the pickled onions, olives, dill, parsley, and tarragon. Set aside.

Whisk together the extra-virgin olive oil and sherry vinegar in a small bowl. Pour over the cucumber and radish mixture and toss to coat. Sprinkle with the sea salt. Set aside.

Spread the poblano-feta dressing on the bottom of each of four plates, dividing it evenly. Place the salad mixture over the top of the poblano-feta dressing, dividing it evenly. Sprinkle with the toasted hazelnuts and feta. Serve immediately.

Sautéed peaches and shishito peppers with goat cheese, cashews, and saffron honey

Peaches and shishito peppers seem an unlikely combination. But the ripe, floral fruit and the mildly peppery Japanese chile both peak in summer and are oddly great together—a little sweet with a little spice. They also make for an interesting textural contrast: one yielding and juicy and the other slightly crunchy. It's easy to get a lot of good charred browning on shishito peppers because they're especially thin-skinned compared with other pepper varieties. The edges of the peaches get nicely caramelized. Creamy, tangy goat cheese goes with the sweetness of the peaches and the smokiness and heat of the shishito peppers. They're mixed with crunchy cashews, and the dish is finished with lemon juice and musky-floral saffron honey.

SERVES 4

¼ cup [35 g] whole cashews

2 Tbsp butter

5 ripe peaches, pitted and cut into wedges

1 cup [70 g] shishito peppers

Salt

Juice of ½ lemon

⅓ cup [5 g] fresh parsley leaves

⅓ cup [4 g] fresh chervil

⅓ cup [4 g] fresh tarragon leaves

3 Tbsp crumbled fresh goat cheese

½ Tbsp saffron honey (page 33)

Heat the oven to 350°F [180°C]. Spread the nuts in a single layer on a small baking dish and place on a middle rack in the oven. Roast, stirring the nuts once for even cooking, until toasty and fragrant, 12 to 15 minutes. Remove from the oven. When cool enough to handle, coarsely chop and set aside.

Heat the butter in a frying pan over medium-high heat. When the butter melts and begins to foam, add the peaches and shishito peppers and sear, turning once with a spatula, until the edges are well browned, 3 to 4 minutes.

cont'd

Pour off the butter from the pan and transfer the peaches and shishito peppers to a bowl. Toss with a pinch of salt and half of the lemon juice. Transfer half of the peaches and shishito peppers to a platter and sprinkle with half of each of the parsley, chervil, tarragon, cashews, and goat cheese.

Top with the remaining peaches and shishito peppers and sprinkle the remaining parsley, chervil, tarragon, cashews, and goat cheese on top. Drizzle with the remaining lemon juice and saffron honey. Serve immediately.

Orange-scented creamed spigarello with almonds and Aleppo pepper

Spigarello has long, thin stems and twisty, curled green leaves and is mildly sweet (not as bitter as its cousins broccoli or rapini). Sometimes called leaf broccoli, spigarello is native to southern Italy but is available in Southern California, its only significant growing region outside of Italy. It shows up here seasonally at farmers' markets. But if you can't find spigarello, you could substitute Tuscan black kale. (Spigarello's flavor reminds me of a cross between broccoli and black kale.) I like spigarello's texture when sautéed: the stems become more tender but still have snap, and the leaves are supple. Adding a little orange-scented cream makes it especially good. In the spring I might add a few radish flowers.

NOTE: You can substitute Aleppo pepper with any coarsely ground, dried, mildly spicy chile, such as New Mexico chile, urfa biber, or cascabel.

SERVES 4

¼ cup [35 g] whole almonds

3 Tbsp avocado or olive oil

2 garlic cloves, cut into thin slices

2 bunches spigarello, about 12 oz [340 g] total, trimmed

¼ tsp salt

½ cup [120 ml] heavy cream

1½ tsp grated orange zest

½ tsp Aleppo pepper

¼ tsp toasted white sesame seeds

Heat the oven to 350°F [180°C]. Spread the almonds in a single layer on a baking sheet and place on a middle rack in the oven. Roast, stirring the nuts once for even cooking, until toasty and fragrant, about 12 minutes. Remove from the oven. When cool enough to handle, coarsely chop and set aside.

Heat the oil in a frying pan over medium heat until hot and shimmering. Sauté the garlic, stirring constantly, until fragrant and it begins to color, about 30 seconds. Add the spigarello and salt and sauté, stirring occasionally, until wilted, 1 to 2 minutes. Add the cream and 1 tsp of the orange zest and cook until the cream reduces slightly and coats the vegetables, about 1 minute. Remove from the heat.

Transfer to a platter. Sprinkle the spigarello with the Aleppo pepper, sesame seeds, toasted almonds, and remaining ½ tsp orange zest. Serve immediately.

Eggplant purée with sumac and garlic

I can't think of anything else like the collapsed, melting interior of roasted eggplant. Tender and rich, it makes the delicious, creamy Middle Eastern dips baba ghanoush and moutabal. These are traditionally made with eggplants that have been roasted over an open flame—best if they are cooked slowly. But this is the quick version. I use Japanese eggplants because they're smaller and cook faster. These are sliced, charred on the stove, then roasted in the oven. There's no peeling necessary, so I get to incorporate the toasted eggplant skins for an even more flavorful dip.

NOTE: I use Japanese sesame paste, labeled atari goma, which can be found at Japanese markets and online. It can be substituted with high-quality unsalted tahini.

MAKES ABOUT 1¼ CUPS [300 G]

3 Japanese eggplants, about 9 oz [250 g] total

3 Tbsp avocado or olive oil

3 garlic cloves, cut into thin slices

1 Tbsp lebni or Greek yogurt

½ Tbsp sesame paste

1 Tbsp ground sumac

⅛ tsp piment d'Espelette

½ Tbsp fresh lemon juice

½ tsp salt

Heat the oven to 400°F [200°C].

Cut the eggplants crosswise into ½-in [12-mm] slices, discarding the stem ends. Heat the oil in a large cast-iron frying pan over medium-high heat until hot and shimmering. Add the eggplant slices and sauté, shaking the pan occasionally, until the edges brown, about 3 minutes. Flip the eggplant slices using a fork or offset spatula, then immediately transfer the pan to the oven.

Roast the eggplant until cooked through and soft, about 10 minutes. Halfway through cooking, rotate the pan and add the garlic, scattering it among the eggplant slices. Remove from the oven and transfer the eggplant to the bowl of a food processor.

Add the lebni, sesame paste, sumac, piment d'Espelette, lemon juice, and salt to the food processor and pulse to a coarse purée. Serve immediately or store covered in the refrigerator for up to 3 days.

Fava "hummus" with mint and Pecorino cheese

The buttery texture and nutty flavor of fresh, fat fava beans make them especially good for "hummus," a coarse purée mixed with garlic, sesame paste, and lemon. I know this isn't hummus per se, but the fava beans are a good stand-in for chickpeas. And the combination of fava beans, sheep's milk cheese, lemon juice, and mint is especially springlike.

NOTE: To shell fava beans, open the pods along their seams and remove the beans. Blanch them in boiling water for 30 seconds and transfer them to an ice bath to stop the cooking. Slip off the waxy coating.

MAKES ABOUT 1¼ CUPS [300 G]

1½ cups [200 g] peeled shelled fava beans (from about 3¾ lb [1,700 g] fava pods)

¼ cup [30 g] grated Pecorino cheese

¼ cup [4 g] fresh mint leaves

Grated zest of ½ lemon

1 tsp fresh lemon juice

2 Tbsp olive oil

Prepare an ice bath by filling a large bowl with ice water. Set aside. Bring a medium saucepan of salted water to a rolling boil over high heat. Add the fava beans and blanch until bright green and al dente, about 1 minute. Drain the fava beans and transfer to the ice bath to cool.

Drain the fava beans again and put them in a food processor. Add the Pecorino, mint, lemon zest, and lemon juice and pulse until blended. Drizzle in the olive oil as you continue to pulse to a coarse purée. Serve immediately or store in a covered container in the refrigerator for up to 2 days.

Lebni with eggplant purée, fava "hummus," and za'atar

Lebni swirled with za'atar, olive oil, sumac, piment d'Espelette, and mint is delicious served with torn flatbread for scooping up all of the thick, creamy yogurt and spices. This dip can be served with fresh fava "hummus" and lightly smoky eggplant purée. You could make and serve any of these components by itself or in any combination. Together, the spices and herbs contrast with the tart yogurt and the slightly sweet fava "hummus" and eggplant purée. At Bäco Mercat, the dish is served with Bäco bread (page 176) smeared with chimichurri (page 84), because I like the surprise of those extra layers of flavor, punctuated by peppery, anise-like parsley and aromatic garlic. Sesame seeds add a little nutty crunch. Serve any extra eggplant purée and fava "hummus" on the side.

SERVES 4

1½ tsp white sesame seeds

1 cup [280 g] lebni or 1 cup [270 g] Greek yogurt

5 Tbsp [75 g] eggplant purée with sumac and garlic (page 226)

5 Tbsp [75 g] fava "hummus" with mint and Pecorino cheese (page 227)

¼ cup [30 g] za'atar

¼ cup [60 ml] extra-virgin olive oil

¼ tsp flaky sea salt

¼ tsp piment d'Espelette

¼ tsp ground sumac

1 Tbsp torn fresh mint leaves

Bäco bread (page 176), toasted bread, or crudités (page 114) for serving

Toast the sesame seeds in a small, dry frying pan over medium heat, stirring frequently, until golden brown and fragrant, about 1 minute. Set aside.

Smear the lebni on a platter, then put the eggplant purée on top of one side of the lebni and the fava "hummus" on top of the other side of the lebni.

Mix the za'atar and olive oil in a small bowl and drizzle all over the plate. Sprinkle with the sea salt, piment d'Espelette, sumac, mint, and toasted sesame seeds.

Serve immediately with flatbread, toasted bread, or crudités.

Imjadra with cherries, parsley, sumac yogurt, and fried shallots

This is a version of the Lebanese dish of simpatico bulgur and lentils. It's similar to mujaddara, which is typically made with rice and lentils, seasoned with cumin or coriander, and topped with fried onions along with melted butter and yogurt. (The ubiquitous kushari in Egypt is rice, lentils, and macaroni with baharat-spiced tomato sauce and fried onions.) Both mujaddara and imjadra are traditionally made with brown or green lentils. I use plump black beluga lentils for their color, mild flavor, and firmer texture. Imjadra is great as a side dish for roasted or grilled meats, but it's also satisfying enough to eat on its own or with just a salad. I add cherries or wedges of summer-ripe plums here because they are meaty and their sweet-tartness balances the earthiness of lentils and bulgur.

SERVES 4

2 tsp cumin seeds

5 Tbsp [80 ml] avocado or olive oil

¼ yellow onion, minced

4 garlic cloves, finely chopped

1 cup [220 g] beluga lentils

Salt

8 cups [1.9 ml] water

½ cup [100 g] bulgur

1 sprig thyme

3 shallots, cut into thin slices

¼ cup [70 g] plain yogurt

¼ tsp ground sumac

½ tsp freshly ground white pepper

¼ tsp cinnamon

½ bunch parsley, leaves only, chopped

Juice of ½ lemon

½ cup stemmed pitted cherries, torn into pieces, or 3 ripe plums, pitted and cut into wedges

¼ cup [7 g] fresh nasturtium or mint leaves (optional)

cont'd

Toast the cumin seeds in a small, dry frying pan over medium heat, stirring occasionally, until fragrant, 2 to 3 minutes. Grind to a fine powder in a spice grinder or with a mortar and pestle. Set aside.

Heat 1 Tbsp of the oil in a frying pan over medium heat until hot and shimmering. Add the onion and half of the garlic and sweat until the onions are soft and translucent, 5 to 7 minutes. Add the lentils, a pinch of salt, and half of the ground cumin, stir to coat, and cook the lentils until toasted, about 5 minutes.

Add 4 cups [950 ml] of the water, turn the heat to medium-high, and simmer, adjusting the heat as necessary, until the lentils are just tender, about 30 minutes. Remove from the heat, drain, and set aside.

Meanwhile, bring the remaining 4 cups [950 ml] water to a boil in a saucepan over high heat. Put the bulgur, ½ tsp salt, and thyme in a large heatproof bowl and pour the boiling water over the grains. Cover tightly with plastic wrap and let stand until the bulgur is tender, about 10 minutes. Drain the excess water and discard the thyme. Set aside.

Line a plate with paper towels. Heat 3 Tbsp of the oil in a saucepan over medium-high heat until hot and shimmering. Add the shallots and cook, stirring occasionally, until golden brown and crispy, about 8 minutes. Remove the shallots from the pan with a slotted spoon and place on the paper towel–lined plate to drain. Set aside.

Mix the yogurt and sumac in a small bowl until combined. Set aside.

Heat the remaining 1 Tbsp oil in a frying pan over medium-high heat until hot and shimmering. Sauté the remaining garlic for just a few seconds, until fragrant. Add the cooked lentils, bulgur, white pepper, cinnamon, and remaining cumin and sauté until hot, 4 to 5 minutes. Remove from the heat. Add the parsley, ¼ tsp salt, and half of the lemon juice and stir to mix. Fold in the cherries.

Transfer to a platter and sprinkle with the remaining lemon juice. Top with the sumac yogurt and fried shallots. Scatter the nasturtium leaves over the top, if desired. Serve immediately.

Braised chicken with leeks, tomatoes, berberé, thyme, and yogurt

This oven-braised chicken is inspired by the Ethiopian stew doro wat, seasoned with the spice mixture berberé and cooked with a lot of leeks rather than the traditional dry-sautéed onions. Bright tomatoes, spicy ginger and chiles, and tart sumac meld with the leeks for a curry-like dish. Rather than stewing on the stovetop, it goes into the oven for a gentler braise. Each bowl gets swirled with creamy, lemony yogurt and garnished with crunchy, nutty sesame seeds. Earthy, floral thyme is sprinkled in at the end. I think of this dish as East Africa meets the Middle East meets the South of France.

SERVES 4 TO 6

2 leeks, trimmed

2 tomatoes

2 lb [910 g] boneless, skinless chicken thighs, cut into 2-in [5-cm] chunks

1 Tbsp berberé (page 36)

1½ tsp ground sumac

Salt

¼ cup [60 ml] avocado or olive oil

1 Tbsp chopped garlic

1 cup [240 ml] chicken or vegetable broth, plus more as needed

1 cup [240 ml] dry white wine

1 Tbsp grated peeled fresh ginger

3 Thai chiles, cut crosswise into thin slices

1 tsp harrough (page 42) or red pepper flakes

3 Tbsp plain yogurt

2 Tbsp water

1 tsp fresh lemon juice

2 Tbsp white sesame seeds

2 Tbsp fresh thyme leaves

Heat the oven to 350°F [180°C].

Cut the leeks in half lengthwise, then cut them crosswise into ¼-in [6-mm] slices. Rinse thoroughly and drain. Set aside.

Grate the tomatoes on the large holes of a box grater into a bowl and discard the skins. Set aside.

Put the chicken in a large bowl and add the berberé, sumac, and 1 tsp salt. Toss until the chicken is seasoned on all sides with the spice mixture. Set aside.

Heat the oil in a large pot or Dutch oven over medium-high heat until hot and shimmering. Add the chicken and sauté until golden brown, 3 to 5 minutes. Add the leeks and sauté until softened, 2 to 3 minutes. Add the garlic and cook, stirring, until fragrant, 1 minute. Add the broth, white wine, tomatoes, ginger, Thai chiles, and harrough, bring to a boil, and cover. Carefully transfer to the oven and bake until the chicken is tender, the broth has reduced slightly, and the flavors have melded, 35 to 45 minutes. Check and taste the broth after about 35 minutes; cook for 10 minutes longer if the flavors need to meld and concentrate further. Depending on the juiciness of your tomatoes, you may need to add ½ to 1 cup [120 to 240 ml] broth or water if the cooking liquid is reducing too quickly.

Remove from the oven. Ladle into bowls. Mix the yogurt, water, lemon juice, and a pinch of salt in a small bowl. Garnish each bowl with a swirl of the lemony yogurt, sesame seeds, and several thyme leaves. Serve immediately.

Creamy grits with blistered tomatoes, pickled serrano chiles, and sunflower-miso tahini

I grew up with grits, and their corn flavor reminded me of the hominy in menudo and my grandmother's pozole, even though they were almost always instant, dressed with butter, brown sugar, and cinnamon. The first time I had hand-milled stone-ground grits was a revelation, with exponentially better taste and texture. I wanted to make a savory grits dish with layers of flavor. So I thought of swirling in a condiment, almost like you would swirl pistou into a soup. Here it's sunflower-miso tahini (page 58)—nutty, umami-rich, and just a little bit sweet. In contrast are the smoky, toasty edges of blistered cherry tomatoes and their burst of tart-sweet juices. Finally, pickled serrano chiles bring sharp-bright heat, acidity, and crunch.

NOTE: Soak the grits overnight. Stone-ground grits have to absorb at least four times their volume in water to become creamy, and this takes time. Anyone who has cooked grits will tell you to stir and stir and stir. But the way I cook grits might be a little unorthodox: Bring them to a boil and then immediately turn off the heat and let them sit for an hour to absorb the water and release their starches. This cuts down the amount of stirring, which helps free up hands in a busy kitchen. Add more water and stir frequently for the final cooking. You can't get away with no stirring at all, not that I know of.

SERVES 4 TO 6

1 cup [90 g] coarse stone-ground grits

4¼ cups [1 L] water

5 Tbsp [70 g] butter, cut into pieces

½ cup [60 g] grated Pecorino cheese

Salt

4 serrano chiles, cut into thin slices

¼ cup [60 ml] distilled white vinegar

2 Tbsp sugar

½ tsp finely chopped shallot

½ tsp finely chopped fresh chives

½ tsp grated lemon zest

12 oz [340 g] cherry tomatoes, preferably Sweet 100s or other vine-ripened variety

2 tsp olive oil

½ to ¾ cup [120 to 180 g] sunflower-miso tahini (page 58)

8 leaves basil, torn

cont'd

Combine the grits and 3 cups [710 ml] of the water in a medium sauce-pan. Cover and let soak at room temperature for several hours. Skim and discard any chaff that has risen to the surface.

Bring the grits (and their soaking water) to a boil, covered, over high heat, then immediately turn off the heat. Let the grits stand, covered, for 1 hour.

Return the saucepan to low heat and add 1 cup [240 ml] water. Cook the grits, stirring occasionally so that they don't stick to the bottom of the pan or burn (try to keep the sides of the pan clean), until porridge-like and creamy, about 30 minutes. Stir in the butter and Pecorino and season with salt to taste. Remove from the heat.

Put the chiles in a heatproof bowl. Put the remaining 1/4 cup [60 ml] water, the vinegar, and the sugar in a saucepan and bring to a boil over high heat. Remove from the heat and carefully pour the boiling vinegar mixture over the chiles. Set aside to cool.

Mix the shallot, chives, and lemon zest in a small bowl. Set aside.

Put the tomatoes in a dry frying pan, drizzle with the oil, and set the pan over high heat. Cook until the tomatoes are charred and burst, 2 to 3 minutes. Sprinkle with ½ tsp salt. Remove from the heat. Add the shallot-chive-zest mixture and toss together.

Divide the grits among shallow bowls. Place the tomato mixture on top of the grits, dividing it evenly. Drizzle 2 to 3 Tbsp of tahini over each bowl and scatter with the torn basil and pickled serrano chiles. Serve immediately.

Nigella-lavender albacore with ume and tomatoes

Albacore tuna is a pretty mild fish, which makes it a good match for a lot of other flavors. The seared crust of sesame seeds, nigella, salt, pepper, and a little lavender is robust enough to stand up to a full-bodied sauce. Because albacore is a summer-season fish, I think of ripe heirloom tomatoes. Their sweet-bright juices pair with tart umeboshi (Japanese pickled plum) in a cream-enriched sauce. I like the added fat (just a little) because albacore is so lean.

NOTE: Because many tuna populations are currently overfished, buy albacore caught in the Pacific with trolls or poles-and-lines. Umeboshi (Japanese pickled plum) is available at Japanese markets and online.

SERVES 4

1½ pints [400 g] cherry tomatoes or 2 large ripe heirloom tomatoes

2 Tbsp avocado or olive oil

2 garlic cloves, chopped

1 Tbsp finely chopped shallot

3 small umeboshi (pickled plums)

8 fresh basil leaves

1 Tbsp heavy cream

1 Tbsp butter

1 tsp fresh lemon juice

Salt

4 sashimi-grade albacore loin fillets, about 5½ oz [155 g] each

Fresh black pepper

3 Tbsp white sesame seeds

1 Tbsp nigella seeds

¼ tsp dried lavender buds

If using large tomatoes, prepare an ice bath by filling a large bowl with ice water. Bring a medium saucepan of water to a boil over high heat. Cut an X in the bottom of each tomato. When the water boils, carefully add the tomatoes and blanch for 30 to 60 seconds. Use a skimmer or slotted spoon to transfer to the ice bath to cool. Drain the tomatoes and peel the skins. Chop the tomatoes, keeping their juices, and set aside.

cont'd

Heat 1 Tbsp of the oil in a frying pan over medium-high heat until hot and shimmering. Add the garlic and shallot and cook, stirring, until fragrant, about 20 seconds. Add the tomatoes (with their juice if using large tomatoes) and cook, pressing on them with a wooden spoon to help break them down, until soft, 3 to 5 minutes. Add the umeboshi, basil, heavy cream, butter, and lemon juice and cook until reduced to a sauce consistency, about 10 minutes. Taste and add a pinch or two of salt, but no more, because the pickled plums are salty. Turn the heat to low and keep warm.

Rinse and pat the albacore dry with paper towels. Season each albacore fillet with ¼ tsp salt and a pinch of black pepper. Mix the sesame seeds, nigella, and lavender on a large plate. Place each fillet on the plate and turn to evenly coat with the nigella-lavender mixture.

Heat the remaining 1 Tbsp oil in a frying pan over high heat until hot and shimmering. Carefully place the coated albacore fillets in the pan and sear until golden brown, about 20 seconds on each side. Remove from the heat and transfer to a cutting surface. Cut the albacore with a sharp knife into large wedges or ¾-in [2-cm] slices across the grain.

Put some of the tomato sauce on each of four plates. Place the albacore on top of the tomato sauce. Serve immediately.

Meat is the most precious ingredient I work with, not because of its price, not because of its flavor, and not because I think it is a better product than vegetables. I value meat because I grew up a butcher's kid, and that means I knew from an early age exactly where meat came from. I understood that a piece of meat on a Styrofoam tray wrapped in plastic was not the whole story.

I was fully aware that steaks came from animals, and I was taught to respect that. So preparing and eating meat comes with responsibility: to buy the best meat possible from a producer who treats animals humanely in a healthful environment, to utilize as much of the animal as possible, and to cook it properly. No pressure!

One of my favorite ways to cook meat is also the easiest: few meals are as welcoming as a celebratory roast. And one of the many great things about a roast is unattended cooking in the oven, which means time for preparing other dishes to go with it.

At the restaurants, I sometimes butcher and prepare whole lambs or pigs, and there are at least one or two large cuts of meat that are weekly specials, sometimes pork shank or côte de boeuf or whole duck. But roasts either big (prime rib) or small (lamb top round) are an occasion, even if it's a Monday night at home.

Whether roasting, slow-roasting, grilling, braising, or sautéing, the end goal is the same: no matter what the cut of meat, it should be tender and juicy. For roasted, grilled, or pan-seared meat, I love a well-browned, flavorful crust and a tender, succulent interior. In general, I prefer medium-rare, because a moist interior with warm flowing juices is directly correlated to the quality and amount of fat and to optimal meaty flavor and texture.

A thermometer comes in handy. Unless you have a lot of experience handling hot meat and can tell doneness by touch, it's an underrated kitchen tool. It makes cooking meat to perfect doneness (whatever doneness you prefer) easy.

Because meat is strong-flavored and densely textured, it can stand up to a lot of bold flavors: spices, herbs, chiles, marinades, rubs. Black pepper is of course a traditional match for the charred crust and sweet-fatty meat of, say, rib eye or lean beef loin. For well-marbled meat black pepper cuts its richness, and for both fatty and lean meat it enhances flavor.

Tellicherry and Lampong black pepper are two favorites for seasoning meat before cooking. They have a robust, almost sweet aroma and a woodsy, floral, sometimes citrusy flavor with a bit of pungent heat.

Black pepper pairs well with so many other seasonings: Black pepper + piment d'Espelette. Black pepper + cumin. Black pepper + rosemary. Black pepper + urfa biber. Black pepper + lemon zest. Black pepper + cacao. Black pepper + coffee. So it's no wonder it's a prominent ingredient in a lot of my favorite spice blends and condiments—baharat, a coffee rub for meat, sweet-and-sour huckleberries, pickled onions, dukkah—which all also happen to go so well with meat.

tender

juicy

CHAPTER

7

peppery

rich

Sichuan pepper lamb top round with English pea and parsley salad

I call lamb top round the win-win cut of meat. From a large muscle of the leg, the top round is typically less than 2 pounds and has all the big flavor of tougher cuts but is tender and succulent. And because it's small, it cooks quickly. It is special enough that you could serve it as a dinner party center-piece but is so easy to handle that it could be a weeknight go-to. Roast it whole, cut it into steaks, or cube it for kebabs. Here it's a roast rubbed with woodsy, tongue-numbing Sichuan peppercorns, and my favorite combination of cumin and coriander—partly inspired by the cumin-laden fried lamb that I love at Sichuan restaurants. Cubeb pepper is the darker, wrinkled berry that looks like black pepper but with a tail. Pungent and slightly bitter, it tastes like a cross between allspice and black pepper.

NOTE: Urfa biber also can be substituted with any coarsely ground, dried, mildly spicy chile, such as New Mexico chile, cascabel, or Aleppo pepper.

SERVES 2 TO 4

2 Tbsp cumin seeds

1 Tbsp coriander seeds

2 tsp Sichuan peppercorns

1 tsp cubeb pepper

1 tsp nigella seeds

½ yellow onion, grated

1 tsp urfa biber or urfa biber shichimi togarashi (page 38)

Fresh black pepper

Salt

1¼ lb [565 g] lamb top round

3 Tbsp avocado or olive oil

1 cup [160 g] shelled English peas

½ small red onion, cut into thin slices

1½ cups [22 g] fresh parsley leaves

¼ cup [4 g] fresh mint leaves

2 Tbsp extra-virgin olive oil

2 tsp sherry vinegar

1 Tbsp fresh lemon juice

cont'd

Heat the oven to 350°F [180°C].

Toast the cumin, coriander, Sichuan peppercorns, cubeb pepper, and nigella in a small, dry frying pan over medium heat, stirring occasionally, until fragrant, 1 to 2 minutes. Grind the spices to a fine powder in a spice grinder or with a mortar and pestle. Sift through a fine-mesh strainer into a large bowl and discard any hulls or stems. Add the grated onion, urfa biber, 3 grinds of black pepper, and ½ tsp salt and stir to combine. Put the lamb in the bowl and rub with the spice mixture so that it covers all sides of the meat. Set aside.

Heat the avocado oil in an oven-safe sauté pan over high heat until hot and shimmering. Add the lamb and sear until all sides are well browned, about 8 minutes. Transfer to the oven and roast until the internal temperature reaches 135°F [60°C] on a meat or instant-read thermometer, about 14 minutes. Remove from the oven and transfer to a platter. Let rest for 10 minutes.

Prepare an ice bath by filling a large bowl with ice water. Bring a pot of salted water to boil over high heat. Add the peas and blanch until tender, about 3 minutes. Drain the peas and transfer to the ice bath to cool. Drain the peas again and transfer to a large bowl. Add the red onion, parsley, mint, extra-virgin olive oil, sherry vinegar, lemon juice, a pinch of salt, and a couple of grinds of black pepper and toss together.

Cut the lamb into slices across the grain and transfer to a platter. Serve immediately with the English pea and parsley salad.

Skirt steak with horseradish yogurt and beets bi tahina

I always got excited when my dad brought home skirt steak from the butcher counter. It usually happened on a weekend, and it always meant grilling fajitas and eating outdoors and a spread that included a lot of tortillas, guacamole, and salsa. Skirt steak is more flavorful than a lot of other cuts of beef and has relatively good marbling even if it isn't the most tender. Two important points about skirt steak: it must be cooked quickly over high heat, and it must be cut properly—across the grain. The quick cooking is a bonus because it means dinner fast. I also like to give the steaks plenty of room in the pan so that it doesn't lose heat and use enough oil that there is even caramelization. (To that end, cook the steaks one at a time; if your pan is large enough to cook two of them, there should be at least an inch between steaks.) Here, skirt steak is seasoned with salt and pepper, seared in a super-hot pan, and basted with butter and thyme. Serve it with spicy horseradish yogurt and beet "hummus," a combination that reminds me of the Polish condiment cwikla.

NOTE: The beets bi tahina and horseradish yogurt can be prepared a day in advance.

SERVES 2 TO 4

HORSERADISH YOGURT

1 cup [270 g] Greek yogurt

1½ Tbsp prepared horseradish

1 Tbsp extra-virgin olive oil

¼ tsp salt

Fresh black pepper

2 skirt steaks, about 1½ lb [680 g] total

1½ tsp salt

1 tsp freshly ground black pepper

2 Tbsp avocado or olive oil

2 Tbsp butter

6 sprigs thyme

2 garlic cloves, crushed

1 cup [220 g] beets bi tahina (page 182)

cont'd

MAKE THE HORSERADISH YOGURT: Mix the Greek yogurt, horseradish, extra-virgin olive oil, salt, and black pepper in a bowl. If not using right away, store in a covered container in the refrigerator for up to 1 day.

Pat the steaks dry with paper towels and season with the salt and black pepper.

Heat 1 Tbsp of the avocado oil in a large frying pan over high heat until the oil is hot and shimmering. Carefully place one of the steaks in the pan and sear for 1 minute. Flip the steak and sear on the second side for 1 minute, then add 1 Tbsp of the butter to the pan, along with 3 of the thyme sprigs and 1 of the crushed garlic cloves.

Carefully tilt the pan slightly to one side and, using a large spoon, continuously baste the steak with the melted butter for 30 seconds. Remove from the heat. Transfer the steak, thyme, and garlic to a plate, loosely cover with aluminum foil, and let rest.

Discard the used oil and butter, wipe the pan clean with a paper towel, and repeat the searing and basting with the remaining avocado oil, butter, thyme, and garlic for the second steak. Remove from the heat and transfer the steak, thyme, and garlic to the plate and loosely cover with the foil. Let rest for 7 minutes.

Cut both steaks into slices across the grain and transfer to a platter. Serve immediately with bowls of the horseradish yogurt and beets bi tahina.

Chicken escabeche with mint

Escabeche is a dish that originated in the Middle East and made its way to Spain via Muslim North Africans, then to Latin America with the conquistadores. Originally a "vinegar stew" called *sikbaj* and made with lamb or seafood (it's the seafood version that caught on), it is supposedly the ancestor of ceviche and fish and chips served with vinegar. The Spanish version of escabeche is typically fried or grilled fish such as tuna or sardines that's then marinated in sherry vinegar and spices for several hours and served chilled. This "escabeche" of pan-roasted chicken is cooked with vinegar, aromatics, spices, and a handful of golden raisins (for a little sweetness), served hot and garnished with lots of fresh fragrant mint.

SERVES 4 TO 6

ESCABECHE MARINADE
1 tsp cumin seeds

1 tsp coriander seeds

¾ cup [180 ml] olive oil

1 yellow onion, cut into fine dice

3 shallots, cut into thin slices

6 garlic cloves, cut into thin slices

1 carrot, peeled and cut into fine dice

1 tsp salt

⅔ cup [160 ml] sherry vinegar

⅓ cup [80 ml] water

1 fresh or dried bay leaf

4 whole chicken legs (thighs separated), about 3½ lb [1.6 kg]

½ Tbsp salt

½ tsp urfa biber, urfa biber shichimi togarashi (page 38), or freshly ground black pepper

2 Tbsp avocado or olive oil

1 serrano chile, cut into thin slices

⅓ cup [65 g] golden raisins

1 cup [16 g] fresh mint leaves

cont'd

Heat the oven to 400°F [200°C].

Warm the cumin and coriander seeds in a dry frying pan over medium-high heat just long enough to start toasting them, about 1 minute, then add 2 Tbsp of the olive oil and heat until hot and shimmering. Add the onion, shallots, garlic, carrot, and salt and sweat, stirring occasionally, until the vegetables are aromatic and softened but do not color, about 3 minutes. Add the vinegar, water, bay leaf, and the remaining oil and bring to a boil over high heat. Lower the heat and simmer for 1 minute. Remove from the heat and set aside.

Sprinkle the chicken evenly with the salt and urfa biber. Heat the 2 Tbsp avocado oil in a wide, heavy-bottomed frying pan over medium-high heat until hot and shimmering. Add the chicken to the pan, skin side down, and sear until very crispy and well browned, 3 to 5 minutes. Flip the pieces of chicken and sear on the second side for 1 minute longer. Remove from the heat.

Pour the marinade over the chicken, scatter the serrano and raisins on top, and transfer to the oven. Bake until the internal temperature of the chicken reaches 165°F [75°C] on a meat or instant-read thermometer, 15 to 20 minutes. Remove from the oven.

Transfer the chicken to a platter. Tear the mint leaves over the marinade in the pan. Spoon the marinade over the meat and serve immediately.

Smoked paprika beef shoulder braised with shiitake-lemongrass broth

I call this a summer braise, because its base is a light broth of dried shiitake mushrooms and lemongrass that's flavorful and fresh. I use it to cook smoked paprika–spiced beef until it is fork-tender. Only during the end of cooking are vegetables added (you can vary the vegetables according to what's in season) so that they remain bright and just on the edge of soft.

NOTE: This makes more shiitake and lemongrass broth than is needed for the recipe. It's good to keep the extra on hand; use it as you would vegetable broth. It can also be kept frozen for several months. Fresh chickpeas are seasonally available at farmers' markets; you can substitute any fresh shelling bean. You can also use the same amount of dried chickpeas that have been soaked over-night; add them to the braise along with the beef.

SERVES 4 TO 6

One 5-in [12-cm] piece lemongrass, cut from the bulb end of the stalk

4 oz [115 g] dried shiitake mushrooms

3 qt [2.8 L] water

2 lb [910 g] beef shoulder, cut into 1½-in [4-cm] cubes

1 Tbsp smoked paprika

1 tsp salt

⅓ cup [80 ml] avocado or olive oil

½ white or yellow onion

2 garlic cloves, sliced

1 tsp cumin seeds

8 oz [230 g] ripe tomatoes or cherry tomatoes, coarsely chopped

5 turnips, peeled and cut into quarters

6 fingerling potatoes, scrubbed but not peeled and cut into ½-in [12-mm] coins

1 cup [155 g] fresh chickpeas

2 cups [40 g] baby kale

Heat the oven to 350°F [180°C].

Trim the lower bulb end of the lemongrass stalk and discard. Cut in half lengthwise and gently bruise the lemongrass stalk with a pestle or the flat side of a chef's knife.

cont'd

Put the lemongrass, shiitake mushrooms, and water in a stockpot and bring to a boil over high heat. Lower the heat and simmer for 1 hour. Remove from the heat, strain carefully, discarding the lemongrass and mushrooms, and set aside.

Meanwhile, place the cubed beef in a large bowl and add the smoked paprika and salt. Toss until the beef is seasoned on all sides with the spice mixture.

Heat the oil in a stockpot or Dutch oven over medium-high heat until hot and shimmering. Add the beef and sear, stirring occasionally, until browned, 2 to 3 minutes. Because the beef is coated in paprika, be careful not to burn it. Add the onion, garlic, and cumin and sweat, stirring occasionally, just to start the cooking process, 2 to 3 minutes. Add the tomatoes and 6 cups [1.4 L] of the shiitake-lemongrass broth.

Cover the stockpot and carefully transfer to the oven. Braise until the beef is fork-tender, about 1 hour 45 minutes. During the last 20 minutes of cooking, carefully add the turnips, potatoes, chickpeas, and baby kale. By the end of cooking, the vegetables should be just tender. Remove from the oven and serve in bowls immediately.

Baharat-spiced porchetta

This is a 10-hour roast. You can put it in the oven early in the morning and have supremely tender pork shoulder by dinner. Carve the porchetta by pulling the meat apart with a fork or cut it into thick slices, and serve it along with your favorite salad or vegetables. It's also a delicious filling for Bäco breads (page 176), along with any number of sauces for even more flavor, and some yogurt sprinkled with sumac. Or serve it with a fresh salad, such as red endive and blood oranges with herbs, blue cheese, dukkah, and Banyuls vinaigrette (page 104). I also have started the porchetta before going to bed, to wake up to pork roast (and have a little for breakfast) and then reheat it later for dinner.

NOTE: Pork shoulder is considered "done" when its internal temperature reaches 145°F [63°C], but it is unctuously tender at about 190°F [90°C] (I admit that when I'm really impatient, I will settle for 170°F [75°C]—but no lower. At this point, it is firm and meaty but still tender and delicious.)

SERVES 4

4½- to 5-lb [2- to 2.3-kg] pork butt, with fat cap

1½ Tbsp salt

2 Tbsp baharat (page 35)

Fresh black pepper

Chimichurri (page 84) or mint and fines herbes salsa verde (page 70) for serving

Heat the oven to 225°F [110°C]. Season the pork by rubbing the salt, baharat, and several grinds of black pepper over the entire roast. Cover loosely with plastic wrap and let the meat rest for at least a couple of hours or up to overnight in the refrigerator.

Place the pork, fat side up, in a roasting pan or 13-by-9-in [33-by-23-cm] baking dish. Cover with aluminum foil. Roast the pork until the internal temperature reaches 190°F [90°C] on a meat or instant-read thermometer, about 10 hours. The meat should be very tender and pull apart easily when you poke at it with a fork. During the last hour or so of cooking, remove the foil so that the top browns.

Let rest for 10 to 15 minutes. To serve, pull the meat apart with a fork, or you can cut it into thick slices. Transfer to a platter. Serve immediately, passing the chimichurri at the table.

Cumin-spiced beef and lamb patties with pine nuts and raisins

These beef and lamb patties remind me of the cumin-spiced lamb skewers of Xinjiang, a region between China, the Middle East, and India. But the addition of pine nuts and raisins is inspired by Sicilian meatballs. There are a lot of ways to serve these: with Bäco bread (page 176) and/or any number of sauces (harissa, kochkocha, or chimichurri, for example); alongside bulgur pancakes (page 193) or mint and fines herbes tabbouleh (see note on page 70), or wrapped in floppy leaves of lettuce. One of my favorite ways is crumbled onto a salad such as Castelfranco with cheddar and miso-fenugreek dressing (page 98).

SERVES 4

1 tsp cardamom seeds

1 tsp cumin seeds

1 tsp anise seeds

1 tsp coriander seeds

1 Tbsp piment d'Espelette

1 Tbsp pine nuts

8 oz [230 g] ground lamb

8 oz [230 g] ground beef

2 tsp salt

15 fresh mint leaves, chopped

15 fresh basil leaves, chopped

2 oz [60 g] feta, crumbled

2 Tbsp golden raisins

1½ Tbsp avocado or olive oil

Toast the cardamom, cumin, anise, and coriander seeds in a small, dry frying pan over medium heat, stirring occasionally, until fragrant, 2 to 3 minutes. Grind the spices to a fine powder in a spice grinder or with a mortar and pestle. Sift through a fine-mesh strainer into a small bowl and discard any hulls or stems. Add the piment d'Espelette and stir to combine. Set aside.

Wipe the pan clean with a paper towel. Add the pine nuts and toast over medium heat, stirring frequently, until browned, about 2 minutes. Remove from the heat and set aside.

In a medium bowl, gently mix the lamb and beef with your hands. Add the ground spices, salt, mint, basil, feta, toasted pine nuts, and raisins and mix until well combined.

Divide the meat mixture into four equal portions and form into patties that are about ½ in [12 mm] thick.

Heat the oil in a large frying pan with a lid over high heat until hot and shimmering. Put the patties in the pan one at a time, giving the pan a little shake after placing each patty so that the meat doesn't stick to the pan. Turn the heat to medium and sear until the bottom is well browned, 1 to 2 minutes. With a spatula, flip the patties one at a time, again giving the pan a little shake after flipping each patty.

Cover the pan with the lid, turn the heat to low, and cook until the patties are medium done, 3 to 5 minutes. Remove from the heat and set aside to rest for 5 minutes. Serve immediately.

tender | juicy | peppery | rich

Lamb and tomato stew with chickpeas and curry leaf Meyer lemon pickle

Inspired by North African tagines, this lamb and tomato stew packs a lot of flavors: mouthwatering tomatoes, fall-off-the-bone lamb, garlic, all the spices in baharat (black pepper, paprika, cumin, coriander, cloves, and cardamom), and pickled lemon. When they're available in the late summer and early fall, fresh green chickpeas can be added to the stew during the last 10 minutes of braising (they cook that fast). Bäco flatbread smeared with herb-packed chimichurri is a good accompaniment for sopping up juicy lamb.

SERVES 4 TO 6

2 lb [910 g] lamb shoulder, cut into 2-in [5-cm] chunks

3 tsp baharat (page 35)

Salt

4 Tbsp [60 ml] avocado or olive oil

4 celery stalks, cut into ¼-in [6-mm] dice

2 yellow or white onions, cut into ¼-in [6-mm] dice

2 poblano chiles, seeded and cut into ¼-in [6-mm] dice

2 carrots, peeled and cut into ¼-in [6-mm] dice

2 bulbs fennel, cut into ½-in [12-mm] dice

2 cups [480 ml] red wine

Two 28-oz [794-g] cans whole tomatoes, puréed with their juice in a blender or food processor

2 cups [480 ml] chicken broth or water

2 bunches cilantro, leaves only

2 heads garlic, halved crosswise

12 slices curry leaf Meyer lemon pickle (page 26) or 1 preserved lemon peel, chopped

1 cup [200 g] dried chickpeas

Bäco bread (page 176, optional) for serving

Heat the oven to 350°F [180°C].

Put the lamb in a large bowl and add 2 tsp of the baharat and 1½ tsp of the salt. Toss until the lamb is seasoned on all sides with the spice mixture.

Heat 2 Tbsp of the oil in a large heavy-bottomed frying pan over medium-high heat until hot and shimmering. Place the lamb in the pan and sear all sides until well browned, about 8 minutes. Remove from the heat, transfer to a plate, and set aside.

Heat the remaining 2 Tbsp oil in a Dutch oven or stockpot with an oven-safe lid over medium heat until hot and shimmering. Add the celery, onions, poblanos, carrots, fennel, and ¾ tsp salt and sweat, stirring occasionally, until the vegetables are aromatic and softened but do not color, 6 to 7 minutes. Add the remaining 1 tsp baharat after 3 minutes.

Carefully pour in the wine and cook until the alcohol has burned off, about 3 minutes. Add the puréed tomatoes, chicken broth, cilantro, garlic, lemon pickle, and chickpeas. Transfer to the oven and braise until the lamb is tender and the meat starts to separate when gently pulled with the tip of a metal spatula, 1½ to 2 hours.

Remove the lamb stew from the oven. Carefully remove the heads of garlic from the stew. Ladle into bowls and serve immediately, along with Bäco bread, if desired.

VARIATION

Lamb neck stew: Lamb neck, a lot like oxtail, is a flavorful cut that braises to melting tenderness. I like serving this stew with one piece of lamb neck per person, which makes for a big portion.

Substitute 3½ lb [1.6 kg] lamb neck (four pieces) for the lamb shoulder. Ask the butcher to trim the lamb neck, leaving just a little of the fat.

Coat the lamb neck pieces with 2 tsp of the baharat and 2 tsp salt. Heat 2 Tbsp oil in a large heavy-bottomed frying pan over medium-high heat until hot and shimmering. Place the lamb neck in the pan and sear until all sides are well browned, 3 to 5 minutes on each side. Remove from the heat, transfer to a plate, and set aside. Proceed as directed in the preceding recipe. The lamb neck is done when tender, 1½ to 2 hours; the meat should easily come away from the bone when pricked with a fork.

To serve, put the lamb neck pieces in each of four large bowls and fill the bowls with the broth.

Berberé double-cut lamb chops

Double-cut lamb chops are twice the fun—more substantial than a single chop, which sometimes seems smallish, and less commitment than the whole rack. Berberé spices are especially delicious with meaty lamb. The spice blend has a little of everything: the four C's (caraway, cumin, coriander, and cardamom) along with Aleppo, allspice, fenugreek, cloves, cubeb, ginger, turmeric, paprika, and cinnamon. As the meat roasts, it fills the kitchen with the aroma of baking spices by way of East Africa.

SERVES 4

Four 2-bone lamb chops, with fat cap, about 11 oz [310 g] each
2 tsp salt
2 Tbsp berberé (page 36)

Heat the oven to 350°F [180°C].

Trim the fat cap on each chop to no more than ¼ in [6 mm] thick. Score the fat cap with the tip of a knife, making shallow diagonal cuts in a diamond pattern with the cuts spaced about 1 in [2.5 cm] apart.

Rub the chops all over with the salt and berberé.

Place the lamb chops fat side down in a large, dry frying pan and set over medium-high heat. (You might have to sear the chops in two batches, depending on the size of your pan.) Sear until the fat is translucent and golden brown, 6 to 8 minutes, carefully spooning out and discarding any excess rendered fat after 3 or 4 minutes (you don't want the chops to fry). While keeping the fat side down, frequently apply moderate pressure on the chops with a spatula to ensure maximum fat-to-pan contact.

Carefully transfer the chops to a rimmed baking sheet with the fat cap facing down. Roast until the internal temperature reaches 127°F to 130°F [53°C to 55°C] for medium-rare on a meat or instant-read thermometer, 20 to 25 minutes. Remove from the oven and transfer to a platter. Loosely cover with aluminum foil and let rest for 10 minutes.

Divide the lamb chops among four plates and serve immediately.

Berberé lamb rack

About 2½ lb [1.2 kg] 8-bone lamb rack
2 Tbsp berberé (page 36)
1½ tsp salt

Heat the oven to 300°F [150°C].

Trim the fat cap to ¼ in [6 mm] thick. Score the fat cap with the tip of a sharp
knife, making shallow diagonal cuts in a diamond pattern with the cuts
spaced about 1 in [2.5 cm] apart.

Rub the meat all over with the berberé and salt.

Place the seasoned lamb rack fat side down in a large, dry frying pan and set
over medium heat. Sear until the fat is translucent and golden brown, 6 to
8 minutes, carefully spooning out and discarding any excess fat after 3 or 4 minutes. While keeping the fat side down, frequently apply moderate pressure
on the chops with a spatula to ensure maximum fat-to-pan contact. Sear the
ends of the rack for 30 to 40 seconds on each side.

Carefully transfer the lamb rack to a rimmed baking sheet with the fat cap
facing down. Roast until the internal temperature reaches 130°F [55°C] for
medium-rare on a meat or instant-read thermometer, about 40 minutes.
Remove from the oven and transfer to a platter. Loosely cover with aluminum foil and let rest for 15 minutes. Slice between the bones for serving.

Whole roasted orange- and soy-glazed duck

The beauty of a roasted duck is its crispy skin and tender meat. This duck is dry-brined for several hours with lots of spices and aromatics. It's then left in the refrigerator, uncovered, for up to 24 hours to dry the skin, so that it can be as crackly as possible. I also score the skin all over the breasts and the legs to render the fat, which helps make it crispy. During the last few minutes of roasting, it's basted with a reduction of orange juice, soy sauce, and baharat, a spice mixture that fortifies the sweet-salty-citrusy glaze.

SERVES 4

¼ tsp cumin seeds

¼ tsp caraway seeds

¼ tsp coriander seeds

1 Tbsp salt

1 garlic clove, finely chopped

1 tsp fresh thyme leaves

1 tsp sugar

½ tsp freshly ground black pepper

⅛ tsp cayenne pepper

4½-lb [2-kg] whole duck

4 cloves

¼ tsp cardamom seeds

½ cup [120 ml] soy sauce

½ cup [120 ml] orange juice

1 Tbsp honey

1 tsp baharat (page 35)

Pinch of red pepper flakes or harrough (page 42)

1 Tbsp butter

Toast the cumin, caraway, and coriander seeds in a small, dry frying pan over medium heat, stirring occasionally, until fragrant, about 2 minutes. Grind the spices to a coarse powder in a spice grinder or with a mortar and pestle.

Mix the ground spices with the salt, garlic, thyme, sugar, black pepper, and cayenne pepper in a bowl or container large enough to hold the duck. Set aside.

cont'd

To score the breast side of the duck, make diagonal slices ¼ in [6 mm] apart with the tip of a very sharp knife, cutting through the skin and fat across the entire breast, but being careful not to cut through to the meat. Turn the bird around and cut slices ¼ in [6 mm] apart in the opposite direction, creating a diamond pattern.

Prick or score the legs all over. Rub the duck all over with the spice seasoning and refrigerate, uncovered, for 4 hours. Rinse the duck to remove the seasoning (otherwise it will be salty) and pat dry with paper towels. Put the duck back in the refrigerator, uncovered, for 12 to 24 hours (preferably 24 hours so that the duck skin is very dry).

Heat the oven to 425°F [220°C]. Put the duck on a rack in a roasting pan, breast side up, and roast for 45 minutes. Carefully turn the duck over so that it's breast side down. Prick around the legs with the tip of a knife or tines of a fork and roast for 45 minutes more.

Turn the duck over again to breast side up, prick the breast and legs, and roast until the skin is crispy, about 40 minutes. This is going to depend a lot on your oven. If it isn't crispy, you can increase the heat to 500°F [260°C] and roast for an additional 10 minutes.

Meanwhile, put the cloves, cardamom seeds, soy sauce, orange juice, honey, baharat, and red pepper flakes in a saucepan and cook over medium-high heat until the mixture is reduced to about 3 Tbsp or ¼ cup [60 ml], about 12 minutes. It will look dry and almost burned. Whisk in the butter until emulsified. Set aside.

During the last several minutes of roasting, brush the entire duck with a very thin layer of the soy-orange glaze (don't use too much or you'll compromise the crispiness). When the skin is crispy, 4 to 6 minutes after the glaze is applied, remove from the oven and let rest for 15 minutes. Transfer to a platter and serve immediately.

Coffee-rubbed prime rib with mint and rose pickled red onions

A standing rib roast of three or four ribs is an automatic dinner party, and a pretty glorious one. I prefer prime rib with a thin layer of the fat cap, which helps prevent moisture evaporation. I'm also a fan of bone-in prime rib because I love the flavors of the fat and meat around the ribs. The spices of the coffee rub penetrate the meat just slightly, but mostly they help create a crust of intensified browning flavors. As sugars in the coffee caramelize, they react with amino acids in the meat, and the spices toast and release their oils. The crust contrasts with the eye of the roast, which is tender and succulent and beefy. Serve it with horseradish yogurt (page 249), mint and rose pickled red onions (page 22), and a vegetable such as blistered green beans with fenugreek-chipotle tomato sauce (page 116).

SERVES 6 TO 8

One 3-rib prime rib roast, about 7 lb [3.2 kg], with ¼-in [6-mm] fat cap

1 Tbsp salt

3 Tbsp coffee-spice rub (page 40)

1 recipe mint and rose pickled red onions (page 22)

Heat the oven to 220°F [105°C].

Trim the fat cap to ¼ in [6 mm] thick. Score the fat cap with the tip of a sharp knife, making shallow diagonal cuts in a diamond pattern with the cuts spaced about 1 in [2.5 cm] apart. Rub the roast all over with the salt and coffee rub. Put the seasoned roast fat side up on a rimmed baking sheet with a wire rack.

Roast the prime rib until the internal temperature reaches 115°F to 118°F [46°C to 48°C], about 2½ hours; rotate the meat after 1 hour. Remove from the oven, loosely cover with aluminum foil, and let rest, fat side down, for 30 minutes; the temperature will continue to rise to about 125°F to 130°F [50°C to 55°C] for medium-rare.

Meanwhile, raise the oven temperature to 450°F [230°C]. Return the roast to the oven for 8 minutes for extra caramelization of the crust (it won't affect doneness). Remove from the oven and transfer to a carving board. You can cut between the bones. Or cut the meat away from the bones, then cut the meat into thinner slices. Transfer to a platter and serve immediately, passing a bowl of the pickled onions at the table.

One of my all-time favorite desserts arrived at the table one cold winter night in Paris at Chez l'Ami Jean: an oversized bowl of light-as-air rice pudding unceremoniously landed in front of me with the business end of a large wooden spoon buried into the middle of it. It was homespun and ethereal at the same time. Sweet and savory. And it was served with a separate bowl of additional whipped cream and another filled with straight salted caramel, which is one of the best things that can happen to a dessert.

These are the kinds of desserts I love the most. They are simple, rustic even, but also have their own elegance and express a sense of generosity. Cups of creamy, quivering panna cotta topped with preserved berries. Handfuls of ripe summer fruit that burst with juices when baked in a crostata.

They have the same intensity and layers of flavor and texture as any savory dish. The quest might be how to make them flakier, silkier, smoother, or creamier, or how to introduce a new flavor or a combination of flavors. I think about how to incorporate many of the elements of other dishes that don't involve sugar: salt, herbs, cheeses, spices, nuts, whole grains. Ultimately, how to balance the sweetness.

Savory, tart, bitter, salty: I like how these offset sugar. My introduction to pastry was the biscuit. It isn't sweet, but it's comforting, rustic, warm, buttery, and flaky. For as long as I've been making desserts, I've been baking biscuits for dessert. I use them for shortcake, and spoon over strawberries mixed into a fool, the British dessert of custard or whipped cream and puréed fruit.

Sometimes the extra savoriness comes from the tartness of crème fraîche or yogurt or sour cream or even pickled fruit, or from the freshness of herbs or the warmth of spice, such as crushed fennel or caraway seeds in a piecrust. Sugar is mitigated by adding whole-grain flour to a dough, or by using matcha, the grassy, bitter Japanese green tea in a dessert.

Caramelized sugar is its own unique phenomenon. When the sugar cooks for a caramel, it becomes dark and complex and savory and just on the edge of bitter, maybe even slightly smoky. Caramel is always good to have on hand, for ice cream especially. Or I'll pour a little cream onto the bottom of a plate, drizzle with some caramel, and then top that with a slice of warm pie or cake.

Like anyone who has had the riz au lait at l'Ami Jean, I couldn't stop thinking about it for a long time. So I make my own version, with Arborio rice and cinnamon and condensed milk, mixed with lots of whipped cream. A bowl of caramel on the side is essential, not just because it's spiked with sea salt. It says there's more to share.

flaky

fruity

caramely

tart

Strawberry-elderflower fool

Elderflower and strawberries say summer (even if fresh elderflower heads are hard to come by in Southern California) in this easy fool, the British dessert that traditionally mixes custard and whipped cream with stewed fruit. This version is whipped cream, jammy berries, and elderflower syrup brightened with a little lemon.

NOTE: Bottled elderflower syrup, or alternatively cordial or liqueur (such as the Bitter Truth elderflower liqueur or St-Germain), is available at select liquor stores and online.

MAKES ABOUT 4 CUPS [630 G] (SERVES 4 TO 6)

4 cups [680 g] fresh strawberries, trimmed and halved
1½ Tbsp fresh lemon juice
3 Tbsp elderflower syrup or cordial
1 Tbsp sugar
Grated zest of ½ lemon
Salt
2 cups [480 ml] heavy cream

Gently mix the strawberries, lemon juice, 2 Tbsp of the elderflower syrup, sugar, lemon zest, and a pinch of salt in a large bowl. Set aside to macerate for 15 minutes.

After 15 minutes, remove 3 cups [510 g] of the macerated strawberries and transfer to a saucepan, reserving the remaining strawberries. Add a pinch of salt and the remaining 1 Tbsp elderflower syrup. Cook the strawberries over medium-low heat until they break down and become jammy, 10 to 12 minutes. Remove from the heat, transfer to another bowl, and set aside in the refrigerator to chill.

Whip the heavy cream with a whisk or an electric mixer in a chilled stainless steel bowl until soft peaks form. Gently fold in the cooked strawberries, just to swirl them through the whipped cream. Then fold in the uncooked strawberries. Spoon the fool into four to six glasses, dividing it evenly. Serve immediately or keep refrigerated for up to 1 day.

Buttermilk wheat biscuit with strawberry-elderflower fool

This is a version of strawberry shortcake, made with biscuits that have a high ratio of whole-wheat flour, along with buttermilk, cream, and plenty of butter. It's what I like best about making biscuits—mixing the dough by pinching the butter with the flour, so that there are uneven shards and beads of it that result in flaky biscuits. If you like flaky desserts but aren't committed to baking pie, biscuits are your friends. Split one open and fill it with a strawberry fool of strawberries macerated with lemon and elderflower cordial. Raspberries would be delicious, too.

SERVES 6

2⅓ cups [280 g] all-purpose flour

1⅓ cups [160 g] whole-wheat flour

2 Tbsp granulated sugar

2 Tbsp baking powder

1 tsp salt

1 cup [230 g] cold butter, cut into ¼-in [6-mm] slices

¾ cup [180 ml] cold heavy cream, plus more for brushing

½ cup [120 ml] buttermilk

1 egg, lightly beaten

1 Tbsp raw sugar

1 recipe strawberry-elderflower fool (page 274)

Heat the oven to 400°F [200°C].

Put the all-purpose flour, whole-wheat flour, granulated sugar, baking powder, and salt in a large bowl and whisk together. Add the cold butter to the flour. Using your fingers, pinch together the pieces of butter and flour so that you get uneven shards and beads of butter (don't work it for too long).

Make a well in the middle of the dough and add the cold cream and buttermilk. Gently mix the dough by hand, folding it until it just comes together. It will be moist but pretty crumbly; press it together to form a small rectangle and cover with plastic wrap. Refrigerate for 1 hour.

cont'd

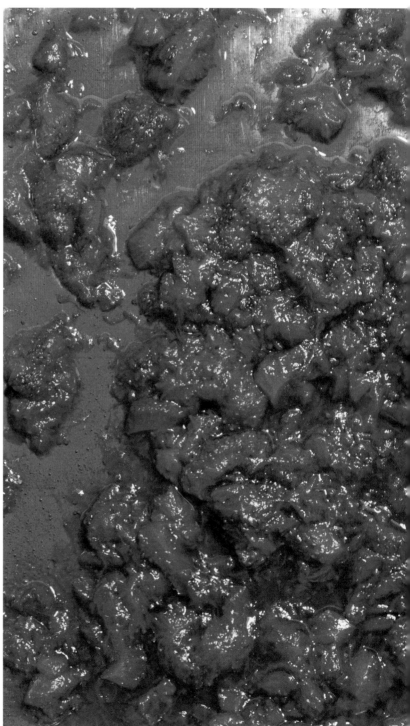

Remove the dough from the refrigerator and transfer to a work surface. Gently roll the dough into a rectangle that's about 10 by 7 in [25 by 17 cm] and ¾ to 1 in [2 to 2.5 cm] thick. Cut out six 3-in [7.5-cm] round biscuits with a biscuit cutter and place on a baking sheet. (You can refrigerate the remaining dough and reroll for more biscuits another time—such as for breakfast.)

Brush the biscuits with the beaten egg and sprinkle over the raw sugar. Bake the biscuits for 10 minutes, then lower the heat to 350°F [180°C] and continue to bake until golden brown, slightly risen, and with visible layers, about 20 minutes longer.

Remove from the oven and cool slightly, then slice the biscuits horizontally. Place the bottom of each biscuit on a plate; divide the fool among the six biscuits, spooning on as much as desired. Cover with the top half of the biscuit. Serve immediately.

VARIATION
Buttermilk-cheddar biscuit: Omit the whole-wheat flour and use 3⅔ cups [440 g] all-purpose flour. Reduce the amount of butter to ¾ cup [170 g]. Add ¾ cup [60 g] grated cheddar cheese along with the cream and buttermilk. Proceed as directed in the preceding recipe.

Salty caramel

This is an all-purpose salty caramel, tinged with the essential oil from orange peel. I serve it alongside rice pudding (page 280) and use it for tarts and upside-down cakes. Drizzle it over ice cream or bread pudding, smear it on waffles, eat it from the spoon.

MAKES 1½ CUPS [355 ML]

1 cup [240 ml] heavy cream
1 cup [200 g] sugar
3 Tbsp butter, cut into 3 pieces
¼ tsp flaky sea salt
1-in- [2.5-cm-] wide strip of orange peel

Put the cream in a small saucepan over low heat to warm.

Put the sugar in a heavy-bottomed saucepan and set over medium-high heat. As it starts to melt (first on the outer edge and then toward the center), don't stir; instead, gently pull the sugar away from the sides of the pan using a heatproof spoon or spatula. Cook the sugar until it becomes a deep amber color, 3 to 5 minutes. Keep a close eye on it; it should be brown, but watch that it doesn't burn.

Carefully whisk in the butter a tablespoon at a time—the hot caramel will froth and steam vigorously. Slowly pour in the warm cream, being careful of the hot steam. Whisk in the salt and orange peel and remove from the heat. Let the orange peel steep in the caramel for 3 to 4 minutes, then carefully remove the orange peel and discard it. Use the caramel as is, or transfer to a jar with a lid and store in the refrigerator for up to 2 weeks (if it lasts that long). Once the salted caramel is cold, you can rewarm it to return it to a pourable consistency.

Canela rice pudding with salty caramel and orange blossom cream

This rice pudding is inspired by the riz au lait at Chez l'Ami Jean in Paris. What was remarkable about it was that, for one, it came served in a huge bowl with a wooden spoon for serving yourself, along with bowls of Chantilly cream and caramel; and two, it was as light as a cloud. It seemed like it was half pudding and half whipped cream. So that's how I make this rice pudding, which is both rich and airy. It gets not only cream but also a little condensed milk. Arborio rice holds its shape even when cooked until it is tender. I add cinnamon to the rice while it's cooking, orange blossom water to the whipped cream, and use roasted almonds as garnish. It has rich, layered flavors and textures.

SERVES 8

½ cup [120 g] Arborio rice

2 cups [480 ml] water

Salt

1 cinnamon stick, preferably Ceylon

4 cups [950 ml] half-and-half, plus more if needed

½ to 1 cup [120 to 240 ml] heavy cream

½ cup [100 g] firmly packed light brown sugar, or to taste

⅓ cup [80 ml] condensed milk

1 tsp vanilla extract

½ cup [70 g] whole almonds

ORANGE BLOSSOM CHANTILLY CREAM

2 cups [480 ml] heavy cream

½ tsp orange blossom water

1 recipe salty caramel (page 279)

Rinse the Arborio rice several times until the water runs clear; this helps the rice cook evenly, with no al dente grains.

Put the water, a pinch of salt, and the cinnamon stick in a heavy-bottomed saucepan and bring to a boil over high heat. Add the rice, lower the heat, and simmer until it has absorbed the water, about 10 minutes.

cont'd

bäco

Stir in the half-and-half and bring the mixture to a boil over medium-high heat. Lower the heat and gently simmer for 30 minutes, stirring occasionally (be sure to scrape the bottom of the pan to prevent the rice from sticking; if it burns, you will have to start over). Depending on how quickly the rice absorbs the liquid, you may need to add a little more water or half-and-half.

Stir in ½ cup [120 ml] of the heavy cream, the brown sugar, condensed milk, and vanilla and continue to gently simmer, stirring frequently, until the rice is very thick and creamy (it should have no "bite" whatsoever), 20 to 30 minutes. Remove from the heat and carefully discard the cinnamon stick.

While the mixture is still very hot, adjust the consistency as needed with additional heavy cream. It should be rather thin; it will thicken dramatically as it cools. Taste the rice and adjust with more salt and/or brown sugar as desired. Transfer to a medium bowl and cover with plastic wrap pressed flat against the surface to prevent a skin from forming. Refrigerate until chilled, 1½ to 2 hours. Store in the refrigerator for up to 3 days.

Meanwhile, roast the almonds. Heat the oven to 350°F [180°C]. Spread the almonds in a single layer on a baking sheet and place on a middle rack in the oven. Roast, stirring the nuts once for even cooking, until toasty and fragrant, about 15 minutes. Remove from the oven and set aside to cool. When cool enough to handle, coarsely chop and set aside.

MAKE THE ORANGE BLOSSOM CREAM: Whip the heavy cream with a whisk or an electric mixer in a chilled stainless steel bowl until soft peaks form. Add the orange blossom water and whip to incorporate. Set aside in the refrigerator to chill.

Spoon the chilled rice pudding into a large bowl and fold in enough orange blossom cream for a fluffy and light consistency (start with 2 cups [120 g] of the whipped cream and add more if desired). Spoon the pudding into bowls. Drizzle with caramel or serve with bowls of caramel and any extra orange blossom cream on the side. Sprinkle with the toasted almonds. Serve immediately.

Pistachio cheesecake custards with matcha sugar and kataifi

Cheesecake enriched with pistachio paste is luscious and nutty and just sweet enough. This one is also light and fluffy, uninterrupted by any crust. I often bake the cheesecake custard in individual custard cups, which they're also served in. This eliminates the hardest part about making a whole cheesecake: waiting for it to chill and set up overnight (but they still have to cool for a couple of hours) and then flipping it onto a platter for presentation. The pistachio flavor is a nod to Middle Eastern desserts, and kataifi—threads of pastry dough—adds buttery crunchiness. But a dusting of Japanese powdered green tea, matcha, takes it in another direction—grassy and pleasantly bitter.

NOTE: Pure pistachio paste is made with only pistachio nuts. It costs more than some other pastes that include sugar and other flavors, but it's worth it for the quality. The color of the paste can vary. (Also, it's a great cheesecake even without the pistachio paste.) You need only a quarter of a 1-lb [455-g] package of kataifi. Cut the kataifi and thaw it in the refrigerator overnight. Take it out of the refrigerator before you start this recipe so that it comes to room temperature.

SERVINGS VARY, DEPENDING ON THE SIZE OF YOUR RAMEKINS

1½ lb [680 g] cream cheese, at room temperature

¾ cup [150 g] granulated sugar

½ tsp salt

⅓ cup [80 ml] water

½ tsp cornstarch

⅓ cup [85 g] pure pistachio paste

⅓ cup [70 g] sour cream

½ tsp vanilla extract

3 eggs plus 2 yolks, at room temperature

4 oz [115 g] thawed kataifi (shredded phyllo dough)

4 Tbsp [60 g] butter, melted

1 tsp matcha

2 tsp powdered sugar

cont'd

Heat the oven to 250°F [120°C].

Put the cream cheese in the bowl of a stand mixer fitted with the paddle attachment and mix on medium-low speed until light and fluffy, about 4 minutes. Stop the mixer, scrape down the sides, and return the mixer to low speed. Slowly rain in the granulated sugar and salt and continue to mix on low speed until incorporated.

Meanwhile, whisk together half of the water with the cornstarch in a medium bowl until smooth. Add the pistachio paste, sour cream, vanilla, and the remaining water and whisk together thoroughly; it should be smooth and glossy.

Stop the mixer and scrape down the sides. Return the mixer to low speed and add the pistachio paste mixture. Gradually turn the speed to medium-high and mix until the pistachio paste mixture is fully incorporated.

Slowly turn the mixer to low speed and add the eggs and yolks, one at a time, until each is incorporated. Stop the mixer and scrape down the sides (and the bottom of the bowl—there is always cream cheese stuck to the bottom), then mix on medium speed one more time to make sure everything is incorporated.

Pour the mixture into individual oven-safe ramekins or custard cups. They can be any size as long as they all fit into one roasting pan or baking dish.

Prepare a water bath: bring a small pot of water to a boil over high heat. Put the ramekins in a roasting pan or other baking dish large enough to hold them all. Then gently pour the boiling water into the roasting pan until it comes halfway up the sides of the ramekins.

Carefully transfer the roasting pan to the oven and bake the custard until it is set but a small circle in the center is still jiggly, about 1 hour 40 minutes. Remove from the oven and let the cheesecakes cool in the roasting pan for 10 minutes.

Remove the cheesecakes from the roasting pan, cover with plastic wrap, and refrigerate for at least 2 hours and up to 2 days.

cont'd

To bake the kataifi, heat the oven to 350°F [180°C]. Unroll the kataifi, pulling it apart and spreading it in a single layer on a baking sheet. Brush all over with the melted butter. Bake until golden brown, about 20 minutes. Remove from the oven, cool slightly, then break the kataifi into 1-in [2.5-cm] pieces or smaller.

Just before serving, sprinkle the kataifi over the cheesecakes. Mix the matcha and powdered sugar together thoroughly. With a fine-mesh sieve, sprinkle the matcha mixture evenly over the top of the cheese-cakes. Serve immediately.

VARIATION
Pistachio cheesecake with matcha sugar

NOTE: If you don't have a springform pan, you can use a glass pie plate in a pinch (line the bottom with parchment paper to flip the cheesecake out, or not).

MAKES ONE 8- OR 9-IN [20- OR 23-CM] CHEESECAKE

Wrap an 8- or 9-in [20- or 23-cm] springform pan in aluminum foil: cut two large pieces of foil and lay them on a work surface in a cross. Set the pan in the middle and fold the edges of the foil up around the sides of the pan.

Make the cheesecake according to the preceding recipe. Pour the mixture into the foil-wrapped springform pan. Prepare a water bath in a roasting pan and bake according to the preceding directions. Bake until the cheese-cake is set and pulls away from the sides of the pan just slightly, about 1 hour 50 minutes. Remove from the oven and let cool for 10 minutes in the roast-ing pan.

Remove the springform pan from the roasting pan and chill the cheesecake in the refrigerator overnight before serving. Run a small knife or metal spatula under hot water. Loosen the sides of the cake by running the knife or spatula along the edge of the cake against the sides of the pan. Release the cake from the springform. Carefully flip the cake onto a board, then flip again onto a cake plate. Sprinkle with the matcha sugar. Slice and serve.

Yogurt panna cotta with pickled huckleberries

The beautiful thing about panna cotta is that it is just sweet enough and just creamy enough, with the right mix of butterfat and gelatin so that it isn't stiff but has quite a bit of jiggle. I use a combination of cream, half-and-half, and yogurt, seasoned with honey and a little salt. The pickled huckleberries make this dessert unexpectedly bright and tart.

NOTE: Gelatin sheets are thin leaves of gelatin film, available at cooking supply stores and online.

MAKES ABOUT 5 CUPS [1.2 L]/SERVINGS VARY DEPENDING ON THE SIZE OF YOUR RAMEKINS

2½ cups [600 ml] heavy cream

1½ cups [355 ml] half-and-half

½ cup [135 g] Greek yogurt

2½ Tbsp sugar

½ tsp salt

1 vanilla bean, split lengthwise

¼ cup [75 g] honey

4½ gelatin sheets

2 cups [480 ml] water

½ cup [105 g] pickled huckleberries (page 29)

Put the heavy cream, half-and-half, yogurt, sugar, and salt in a saucepan over medium-high heat. Scrape the seeds from the vanilla bean with the tip of a knife and add the seeds to the saucepan. Whisk the mixture and heat until hot but not boiling, about 3 minutes. Whisk in the honey and immediately remove from the heat.

Put the gelatin sheets and water in a small bowl and let the gelatin sheets soak until softened, 1 to 2 minutes. Remove from the water and gently squeeze with your hands to remove any excess. Add the gelatin sheets to the warm cream mixture and whisk until thoroughly incorporated.

Spray ramekins or custard cups with nonstick cooking spray. Pour the panna cotta mixture into the ramekins, cover with plastic wrap, and refrigerate until set, at least 5 hours and up to 2 days.

When the panna cotta is set, remove the plastic wrap and, if desired, carefully unmold the panna cotta onto plates. Top each one with a spoonful of the pickled huckleberries. Serve immediately.

Blueberry and frangipane rye-caraway crostata

Rustic crostata is the free-form version of a fruit tart. The appeal is its made-by-hand good looks, the dough folded over a mound of summer fruit. It's always been made with summer fruit, going back to some of the first recipes published in Italian cookbooks in the sixteenth century: plums, peaches, or cherries sprinkled with cinnamon, sugar, and crumbled Neapolitan mostaccioli cookies. Here it's peak-season (early summer) blueberries with a little bit of frangipane, or almond pastry cream. The dough includes a good portion of rye flour and a spoonful of caraway, which gives it a richer flavor and color.

MAKES ONE 12-IN [30.5-CM] CROSTATA

FRANGIPANE

6 Tbsp [85 g] butter, at room temperature

½ cup [100 g] granulated sugar

1 egg

2 tsp brandy

1 cup [100 g] almond meal

2 tsp all-purpose flour

1 tsp cornstarch

DOUGH

1½ tsp caraway seeds

1 cup plus 1 Tbsp [130 g] all-purpose flour

⅓ cup [40 g] rye flour

1 Tbsp granulated sugar

½ tsp salt

6 Tbsp [85 g] cold butter, cut into pieces

2 Tbsp [55 g] cold shortening, cut into pieces

2 Tbsp gin, vodka, or distilled white vinegar

2 Tbsp water

4 cups [440 g] fresh blueberries or 4 cups [650 g] huckleberries

1 egg, lightly beaten

1 Tbsp raw sugar

MAKE THE FRANGIPANE: Put the butter and granulated sugar in the bowl of a stand mixer fitted with the whisk attachment and mix on medium speed until smooth and satiny. Turn the speed to low and add the egg

cont'd

and brandy. Return the mixer to medium speed and mix until incorporated. Stop the mixer and scrape down the sides. Add the almond meal, flour, and cornstarch and mix on medium speed until well incorporated. Transfer the mixture to a covered container and refrigerate for 1 hour and up to 2 days (soften at room temperature).

MAKE THE DOUGH: Toast the caraway seeds in a small, dry frying pan over medium heat, stirring occasionally, until golden brown and fragrant, 2 minutes. Grind to a fine powder in a spice grinder or with a mortar and pestle. Sift through a fine-mesh strainer into a bowl and discard any hulls.

Put the all-purpose flour, rye flour, granulated sugar, toasted caraway, and salt in the clean bowl of a stand mixer fitted with the paddle attachment and mix on low speed to combine. Add the butter and mix on medium speed until the mixture is crumbly and the butter is the size of peas (being careful not to overmix). Add the shortening a little at a time and continue to mix for 10 seconds. Add the gin and water and mix until just combined, about 10 seconds. The dough will be fairly soft.

Turn the dough out onto a floured work surface and gather into a ball; flatten into a disk and cover it in plastic wrap. Refrigerate for at least 30 minutes and up to 2 days.

When ready to bake, remove the dough from the refrigerator and let it sit at room temperature for about 10 minutes. Line a baking sheet with parchment paper. Unwrap the dough and roll it out on a floured work surface into a 14-in [35.5-cm] circle. Flour the dough and fold it in half. Carefully transfer the dough to the parchment-lined baking sheet, then unfold. Return it to the refrigerator for 15 minutes.

Heat the oven to 375°F [190°C].

Remove the dough from the refrigerator and spread the frangipane in the center, leaving a 4-in [10-cm] border of exposed dough. Fill the center with the blueberries, then brush some of the beaten egg onto the exposed dough border. Gently fold the border of the pastry over the fruit, pleating the dough every 2 in [5 cm]. Thoroughly brush the entire outer edge of the dough with beaten egg and sprinkle with raw sugar.

Bake until the pastry is well browned, 1 hour to 1 hour 15 minutes. Remove from the oven and let cool for 20 minutes. Slice and serve immediately.

Blackberry sesame cake with cardamom sugar

I use Japanese sesame paste in this cake instead of tahini. I've found that it's often less bitter than many brands of tahini. The nutty, toasty sesame paste is mixed with a little bit of sugar and salt and drizzled on top of the cake along with cardamom-infused sugar. As the cake bakes, the sesame paste and cardamom sugar become crystallized and almost caramely, with a nice, almost savory crunch—a good contrast to the moist cake.

MAKES ONE 9-IN [23-CM] LOAF CAKE

⅛ tsp cardamom seeds

1 cup [200 g] plus 1½ Tbsp sugar

2⅓ cups [280 g] flour

1 Tbsp baking powder

Salt

2 eggs

1 cup [270 g] plain yogurt

½ cup [120 ml] avocado or vegetable oil

2 cups [340 g] fresh blackberries

¼ cup [35 g] sesame paste

Heat the oven to 350°F [180°C]. Line a pain de mie or loaf pan with parchment paper, then butter and flour the bottom and sides.

Toast the cardamom seeds in a small, dry frying pan over medium heat, stirring occasionally, until fragrant, 1 to 2 minutes. Grind the seeds to a fine powder in a spice grinder or using a mortar and pestle. Mix with 1½ tsp of the sugar in a small bowl and set aside.

Sift the flour, baking powder, and ¼ tsp salt into another bowl. Mix the eggs, yogurt, 1 cup [200 g] sugar, and the oil with a wooden spoon in a large bowl. Add the flour mixture and stir to combine. Gently fold in the blackberries, then transfer the batter into the pan.

Mix the remaining 1 Tbsp sugar, a pinch of salt, and the sesame paste in a small bowl until blended; spread the sesame paste mixture all over the top of the cake and sprinkle with the cardamom sugar.

Bake until a knife or cake tester inserted into the center of the cake comes out clean (the internal temperature should be about 205°F [95°C]), about 1 hour. Remove from the oven and cool completely, then remove from the pan. Slice and serve warm or at room temperature. Store, covered in plastic wrap, for up to 2 days.

Acidity and thirst-quenching zing: that's what I'm looking for in a tonic drink. When working on the line, like a lot of other professional cooks, I resort to drinking from a plastic deli container—what's known as the deli cup. It isn't glamorous, but it does the job (of being easy to grab and not breakable in a busy, crowded kitchen). Instead of ice water, mine's usually filled with a mix of fresh ginger syrup, lime juice, and bubbly soda water.

Syrup made from the knobby, fragrant rhizome ginger is the base for a lot of my favorite drinks. It's fresh, aromatic, and spicy, a little citrusy, floral, and peppery. The active ingredient in ginger that gives it its kick is gingerol, which is related to capsaicin in chiles and piperine in black pepper. It makes ginger's flavor come into laser-sharp focus, which is why ginger seems to make other ingredients more vivid and zingy.

At Bar Amá, fresh ginger syrup is used in cocktails but also nonalcoholic drinks called fruit mashes, because the intense syrup is mixed with muddled fruit—whatever is in season. Ginger's distinct flavor goes with almost any fruit we can throw at it: pineapple, cherry, orange, lime, lemon, passion fruit, mango, strawberry, prickly pear. And it's great with herbs, too; I use mainly mint and tarragon. Most importantly, the spicy heat of ginger balances sweetness.

I don't like overly sweet drinks but do love fruit (which can often be sweet). So ginger, spices, herbs, and acidity are a counterbalance. That's why I like ginger so much. And the vinegar in sweet-and-sour shrubs. Shrubs are concentrated syrups made from vinegar and fruit or vegetable juice (and sometimes alcohol). They're both tart and sweet, and they simultaneously quench your thirst and stimulate your appetite. And the acidity makes them a good match for food with bold flavors. They're added to cocktails, or served topped with fizzy water as punchy sodas.

Shrubs have their roots in the tradition of fruit preservation, back to Persian sharbet, a mixture of fruit juice, spices, herbs, nuts, flowers, and other flavorings added to water. The potential flavor combinations seem inexhaustible. I've been through a lot of them: Thai basil and lemon, apricot and rose geranium, cherry and tarragon, grapefruit and dill . . . The syrups are fun to make and can be kept for weeks. Just add soda water for a refreshing drink.

I like tangy yogurt drinks for the same reason I like shrubs: their acidity. But also because they add another level of savoriness with just enough richness. They aren't too thick, blended with ice and juices and herbs and spices. And a tiny bit of salt. Worthy of a real glass.

bubbly

sweet

sour

vivid

Yogurt drinks

These drinks are inspired by the yogurt beverages of the Middle East and South Asia, such as ayran, doogh, and lassi. Tangy yogurt is refreshing, and there's just enough in these recipes to make a beverage that's a little bit (not overly) creamy. Yogurt along with ice, effervescent soda water, fruit, nuts, herbs, and/or spices is a thirst-quenching combination. These aren't thick smoothies, but are icy, fruity, tart, and bubbly.

Sudachi-cucumber yogurt drink

NOTE: Sudachi is the lime-like Japanese citrus that arrives in California in late summer or early fall. Its flavor is like a lime that's just slightly spicy (with the aromas of pepper and cumin). If you can't find the Japanese sour citrus sudachi, use a combination of fresh lemon (or Meyer lemon) and lime juice.

SERVES 1

1 cucumber
1 generous cup [150 g] ice cubes
1 cup [240 ml] soda water
½ cup [135 g] plain yogurt
3 Tbsp fresh sudachi juice
1½ Tbsp sugar
Pinch of salt

Juice the cucumber with an electric juicer or juice extractor and strain the juice into a saucepan. You should have 1 cup [120 ml] cucumber juice.

Blend the cucumber juice, ice cubes, soda water, yogurt, sudachi juice, sugar, and salt in a blender until well combined. Pour into a glass and serve immediately.

Watermelon-lime–white pepper yogurt drink

SERVES 1

1½ cups [210 g] cubed watermelon, 1-in [2.5-cm] cubes
1 generous cup [150 g] ice cubes
1 cup [240 ml] soda water
½ cup [135 g] plain yogurt
¼ cup [60 ml] fresh lime juice
2 Tbsp honey
⅛ tsp white pepper
Pinch of salt

Blend the watermelon, ice cubes, soda water, yogurt, lime juice, honey, white pepper, and salt in a blender until well combined. Pour into a glass and serve immediately.

Rosewater-pistachio yogurt drink

SERVES 1

⅓ cup [50 g] shelled raw pistachios
1 generous cup [150 g] ice cubes
1 cup [240 ml] soda water
½ cup [135 g] plain yogurt
1½ Tbsp honey
¼ tsp rosewater
Pinch of salt

Heat the oven to 350°F [180°C]. Spread the pistachios in a single layer in a small baking dish and place on a middle rack in the oven. Roast, stirring the nuts once for even cooking, until toasty and fragrant, about 10 minutes. Set aside to cool.

Once cool enough to handle, put the pistachios in a blender. Blend with the ice cubes, soda water, yogurt, honey, rosewater, and salt until well combined. Pour into a glass and serve immediately.

Tangerine-mint yogurt drink

SERVES 1

1 cup [240 ml] tangerine juice (from about 3 tangerines)
1 generous cup [150 g] ice cubes
1 cup [240 ml] soda water
½ cup [135 g] plain yogurt
2 Tbsp ginger syrup (page 302)
5 fresh mint leaves
Pinch of salt

Blend the tangerine juice, ice cubes, soda water, yogurt, ginger syrup, mint, and salt in a blender until well combined. Pour into a glass and serve immediately.

Fruit mashes

The bar at Bar Amá serves nonalcoholic "fruit mashes," prepared with a base of strong ginger syrup, lemon juice, and muddled fresh pineapple. To that are added other fruit and herbs. Once muddled, all of those herbs and fresh fruit are left in the glass.

Ginger syrup

1 lb [455 g] peeled fresh ginger
1¼ cups [250 g] sugar

Juice the ginger with an electric juicer or juice extractor and strain the juice into a saucepan. You should have about 1¼ cups [300 ml] juice. Add the sugar and bring to a boil over high heat. Boil the mixture, stirring occasionally, until the sugar has completely dissolved, about 4 minutes. Store in a lidded jar in the refrigerator for up to 5 days or in a sealed container in the freezer for up to 1 month.

Cherry-mint fruit mash

SERVES 1

⅓ cup [40 g] diced pineapple
6 pitted cherries
6 fresh mint leaves
1 Tbsp ginger syrup (recipe above)
1½ tsp fresh lemon juice
½ cup [120 ml] soda water

Muddle the pineapple, cherries, and mint leaves in a glass. Stir in the ginger syrup and lemon juice. Top with soda water and serve immediately.

Blackberry–Thai basil fruit mash

SERVES 1

⅓ cup [40 g] diced pineapple

8 blackberries

6 fresh Thai basil leaves or 4 fresh regular basil leaves

1 Tbsp ginger syrup (facing page)

1½ tsp fresh lemon juice

½ cup [120 ml] soda water

Muddle the pineapple, blackberries, and Thai basil in a glass. Stir in the ginger syrup and lemon juice. Top with soda water and serve immediately.

Strawberry-tarragon fruit mash

SERVES 1

⅓ cup [40 g] diced pineapple

4 fresh strawberries

6 fresh tarragon leaves

1 Tbsp ginger syrup (facing page)

1½ tsp fresh lemon juice

½ cup [120 ml] soda water

Muddle the pineapple, strawberries, and tarragon in a glass. Stir in the ginger syrup and lemon juice. Top with soda water and serve immediately.

Shrub-and-sodas

I use tart-sweet shrubs, a concentrate of vinegar and fruit, to mix with soda water for nonalcoholic tonics. These go great with boldly flavored food, thanks to their bright acidity. The spectrum of flavor combinations is vast, and each is intensified by apple cider vinegar. The following recipes are a sampling of the revolving flavors of shrubs served at Bäco Mercat. Shrubs are easy to make at home and great to have on hand for cocktails, too.

Pour 2 Tbsp [1 oz/30 ml] of shrub (recipes follow) into a glass and add ¾ cup [180 ml] of soda water, the bubblier the better. Add ice. Serve immediately.

Celery shrub

MAKES 1 CUP [240 ML]

3 Tbsp celery seeds
1 cup [240 ml] apple cider vinegar
2 celery stalks, cut into ½-in [12-mm] slices
½ cup [100 g] sugar

Toast the celery seeds in a dry saucepan over medium-high heat until fragrant, about 45 seconds. Add the apple cider vinegar and celery and bring to a boil over high heat. Remove from the heat. Cool, transfer to a covered container, and refrigerate for 3 days to meld the flavors.

Put the unstrained mixture in a saucepan. Add the sugar and bring to a boil over high heat. Boil, whisking occasionally, until the sugar is dissolved. Carefully strain the shrub, discarding the solids, and pour it into a heatproof jar with a lid; cool uncovered. Once cool, store with the lid on for 2 weeks in the refrigerator.

VARIATION
Celery-cucumber shrub-and-soda: Muddle two 1-in [2.5-cm] slices of cucumber in a glass. Add 2 Tbsp [1 oz/30 ml] celery shrub and ice. Add ¾ cup [180 ml] soda water and serve immediately.

Grapefruit-dill shrub

MAKES 1 CUP [240 ML]

1 grapefruit
1 cup [240 ml] apple cider vinegar
1 dill sprig, fronds only
¾ cup [150 g] sugar

Remove the peel and pith of the grapefruit and coarsely chop the fruit. Put it in a saucepan with the apple cider vinegar and bring to a boil over high heat. Remove from the heat and add the dill. Cool, transfer to a covered container, and refrigerate for 3 days to meld the flavors.

Strain the liquid into a saucepan; you should have ¾ cup [180 ml]. Add the sugar and bring to a boil over high heat. Boil, whisking occasionally, until the sugar is dissolved, about 1 minute. Carefully pour it into a heatproof jar with a lid; cool uncovered. Once cool, store with the lid on for 2 weeks in the refrigerator.

Peach-sumac shrub

MAKES 1 CUP [240 ML]

One 10-oz [295-g] ripe peach, pitted
1 cup [240 ml] apple cider vinegar
2 Tbsp ground sumac
⅓ cup [65 g] sugar

Put the peach and apple cider vinegar in a saucepan and bring to a boil over high heat. Add the sumac. Immediately remove from the heat. Cool, transfer to a covered container, and refrigerate for 3 days to meld the flavors.

Strain the liquid into a saucepan; you should have ¾ cup [180 ml]. Add the sugar and bring to a boil over high heat. Boil, whisking occasionally, until the sugar is dissolved. Carefully pour the shrub into a heatproof jar with a lid; cool uncovered. Once cool, store with the lid on for 2 weeks in the refrigerator.

Index

A

Adjika vinaigrette, 64

Albacore, nigella-lavender, with ume and tomatoes, 241–43

Aleppo pepper, 17

Almonds

blueberry and frangipane rye-caraway crostata, 290–92

breakfast dukkah, coconut, rosebud, and, 51

canela rice pudding with salty caramel and orange blossom cream, 280–82

frangipane, 290–92

mortar-and-pestle romesco, 60

orange-scented creamed spigarello with Aleppo pepper and, 224

salbitxada, 63

and sumac dukkah, 49

"Almostarda," quick cherry, 30

Anchovies

Caesar dressing, 125–26

rutabaga and pancetta with lemon, capers, and, 190–92

walnut-miso bagna cauda, 56

Aonori mascarpone butter, 88

Apple, fennel, kale, and shaved cauliflower with creamy dill dressing and bacon bread crumb persillade, 113

Asian pears

crudités with walnut-miso bagna cauda, 114–15

and snap pea salad with grapefruit, burrata, and hazelnuts, 107–8

Avocados

crudités with walnut-miso bagna cauda, 114–15

eggplant with Persian cucumbers, herbs, cipollini-buttermilk dressing, and, 194–95

ginger-soy dressing, salted cucumbers with, 112

hamachi crudo with adjika, yuzu-dashi vinaigrette, potato croquettes, and, 154–56

B

Bäco bread, 175–79

Bacon. *See also* Pancetta

bread crumb persillade, 55

Bagna cauda, walnut-miso, 56

Baharat, 35

Barley porridge with ginger and sautéed oranges, 212–13

Beans

chickpeas, lamb and tomato stew with curry leaf Meyer lemon pickle and, 262–63

fava "hummus" with mint and Pecorino cheese, 227

green, blistered, with fenugreek-chipotle tomato sauce, 116

Beef

carpaccio, coffee-rubbed, with juniper-tarragon vinaigrette and crispy shallots, 157–58

lengua "schnitzel" with brown butter, capers, and cherry tomatoes, 172–74

meatballs, baked fenugreek-nigella pork and, 135–36

meatballs, berberé-spiced, 136

patties, cumin-spiced lamb and, with pine nuts and raisins, 260–61 prime rib, coffee-rubbed, with mint and rose pickled red onions, 270

shoulder, smoked paprika, braised with shiitake-lemongrass broth, 255–56

skirt steak with horseradish yogurt and beets bi tahina, 249–51

Beets

bi tahina, 182

molasses, pomegranate and, 32

roasted golden, with radishes, cucumbers, hazelnuts, and creamy poblano-feta dressing, 218–20

Berberé, 36

Biscuit, buttermilk wheat, with strawberry-elderflower fool, 276–78

Blackberries

sesame cake with cardamom sugar, 293

–Thai basil fruit mash, 303

Blueberry and frangipane rye-caraway crostata, 290–92

Bonito flakes

dashi concentrate, 76

Bread

Bäco, 175–79

caraway croutons, 54

crumb persillade, bacon, 55

salmorejo, 66

Broccolini

crudités with walnut-miso bagna cauda, 114–15

sautéed, with Mexican sriracha and queso fresco, 134

Brussels sprouts

"Caesar," 125–26

crudités with walnut-miso bagna cauda, 114–15

Bulgur

imjadra with cherries, parsley, sumac yogurt, and fried shallots, 230–32

pancakes with grape leaves, raisins, and goat cheese, 193

Butter, 17

aonori mascarpone, 88

chermou-lata, 69

ghee, 86–87

Buttermilk

-cacik soup, chilled, with dill and walnuts, 214

wheat biscuit with strawberry-elderflower fool, 276–78

C

Cabbage slaw with crème fraîche, mitsuba, and kochkocha, 102

Cacik, 92

-buttermilk soup, chilled, with dill and walnuts, 214

Tuscan melon and Persian cucumber salad with, 110

"Caesar" Brussels sprouts, 125–26

Caesar dressing, 125–26

Cakes. See also Cheesecake

blackberry sesame, with cardamom sugar, 293

Canela rice pudding with salty caramel and orange blossom cream, 280–82

Caramel, salty, 279

Caraway croutons, 54

Cashews

   and coconut breakfast dukkah, 52

   sautéed peaches and shishito peppers with
      goat cheese, saffron honey, and, 221–23

Castelfranco with cheddar and miso-
   fenugreek dressing, 98–99

Cauliflower. *See also* Romanesco

   caramelized, with mint, pine nuts, lime, and
      yogurt, 132–33

   crudités with walnut-miso bagna cauda,
      114–15

   shaved, fennel, kale, and apple with creamy
      dill dressing and bacon bread crumb
      persillade, 113

Celery

   -cucumber shrub-and-soda, 306

   shrub, 306

Chantilly cream, orange blossom, 280–82

Cheese. *See also* Cheesecake

   blue, red endive and blood oranges with
      dukkah, Banyuls vinaigrette, and, 104–6

   burrata, snap pea and Asian pear salad with
      grapefruit, hazelnuts, and, 107–8

   cheddar, Castelfranco with miso-fenugreek
      dressing and, 98–99

   feta, sweet potatoes with aonori
      mascarpone butter, honey, and, 188

   feta-poblano dip, 79

   feta-poblano dressing, creamy, 80

   goat, bulgur pancakes with grape leaves,
      raisins, and, 193

   goat, sautéed peaches and shishito peppers
      with cashews, saffron honey, and, 221–23

   mascarpone butter, aonori, 88

   Pecorino, fava "hummus" with mint and,
      227

Pecorino rice, creamy, berberé chicken and,
   196–98

   ricotta, fresh, 91

Cheesecake

   custards, pistachio, with matcha sugar and
      kataifi, 283–86

   pistachio, with matcha sugar, 286

Chermou-lata, 68–69

   butter, 69

Cherries

   "almostarda," quick, 30

   imjadra with parsley, sumac yogurt, fried
      shallots, and, 230–32

   -mint fruit mash, 302

Chicken

   berberé, and creamy Pecorino rice, 196–98

   braised, with leeks, tomatoes, berberé,
      thyme, and yogurt, 234–35

   escabeche with mint, 252–54

Chickpeas, lamb and tomato stew with curry
   leaf Meyer lemon pickle and, 262–63

Chiles

   adjika vinaigrette, 64

   arbol-guajillo furikake, 39

   berberé, 36

   chimichurri, 84

   harrough, 42–44

   kochkocha, 82

   Mexican sriracha, 85

   mint and fines herbes salsa verde, 70

   mortar-and-pestle harissa, 62

   muhammara, 59

   pickled serrano, 238–40

   poblano-feta dip, 79

poblano-feta dressing, creamy, 80

poblano soup with pancetta and pickled grapes, 216–17

shishito peppers, sautéed peaches and, with goat cheese, cashews, and saffron honey, 221–23

Chimichurri, 84

Citrus and dry-cured olive salad, 163–64

Coconut

breakfast dukkah, cashew and, 52

breakfast dukkah, Marcona almond, rosebud, and, 51

toasting, 45

Coffee

-rubbed beef carpaccio with juniper-tarragon vinaigrette and crispy shallots, 157–58

-rubbed prime rib with mint and rose pickled red onions, 270

-spice rub, 40

Corn

cake, griddled, with aonori mascarpone butter, 144–46

grits, creamy, with blistered tomatoes, pickled serrano chiles, and sunflower-miso tahini, 238–40

pancakes, griddled, with aonori mascarpone butter, 146

Crème fraîche, 94

Croquettes, potato, 151–52

Crostata, blueberry and frangipane rye-caraway, 290–92

Croutons, caraway, 54

Crudités with walnut-miso bagna cauda, 114–15

Cubeb honey, 33

Cucumbers

cacik, 92

-celery shrub-and-soda, 306

eggplant with avocado, herbs, cipollini-buttermilk dressing, and, 194–95

jicama salad with mango, fennel, peanuts, lime and fish sauce vinaigrette, and, 147

roasted golden beets with radishes, hazelnuts, creamy poblano-feta dressing, and, 218–20

salad, Tuscan melon and, with cacik, 110

salted, with avocado ginger-soy dressing, 112

-sudachi yogurt drink, 298

Curry leaf Meyer lemon pickle, 26

Custards, pistachio cheesecake, with matcha sugar and kataifi, 283–86

D

Dashi

concentrate, 76

-yuzu vinaigrette, 77

Dill dressing, creamy, 95

Dips

beets bi tahina, 182

cacik, 92

English pea and dill "hummus," 184

fava "hummus" with mint and Pecorino cheese, 227

lebni with eggplant purée, fava "hummus," and za'atar, 228

poblano-feta, 79

walnut-miso bagna cauda, 56

Dressings. *See also* Vinaigrettes

Caesar, 125–26

cipollini-buttermilk, "broken," 74

dill, creamy, 95

juniper-tarragon tahini, creamy, 73

poblano-feta dressing, creamy, 80

Duck, whole roasted orange- and soy-glazed, 267–68

Dukkah, 45, 53

almond and sumac, 49

cashew and coconut breakfast, 52

hazelnut and fennel, 48

Marcona almond, coconut, and rosebud breakfast, 51

Virginia peanut and coriander, 47

E

Eggplant

with avocado, Persian cucumbers, herbs, and cipollini-buttermilk dressing, 194–95

purée with sumac and garlic, 226

Endive

red, and blood oranges with blue cheese, dukkah, and Banyuls vinaigrette, 104–6

snap pea and Asian pear salad with grapefruit, burrata, and hazelnuts, 107–8

F

Fennel

honey, 33

jicama salad with mango, cucumber, peanuts, lime and fish sauce vinaigrette, and, 147

kale, shaved cauliflower, apple, and, with creamy dill dressing and bacon bread crumb persillade, 113

pollen honey, 33

seeds, toasting, 45

Fish. *See also* Anchovies

albacore, nigella-lavender, with ume and tomatoes, 241–43

hamachi crudo with adjika, yuzu-dashi vinaigrette, avocado, and potato croquettes, 154–56

ocean trout, slow-roasted berberé-cured, with lemon tempura and citrus and olive salad, 166–68

rainbow trout, panfried, with brown butter, Meyer lemon, green olives, and chives, 160–62

Flatbread, Bäco, 175–79

Flour, 17

Flowering choy with lime and fish sauce vinaigrette, 130

Fool, strawberry-elderflower, 274

Frangipane, 290–92

Fruit mashes, 300

blackberry–Thai basil, 303

cherry-mint, 302

strawberry-tarragon, 303

Furikake, arbol-guajillo, 39

G

Gai lan

flowering choy with lime and fish sauce vinaigrette, 130

Ghee, 86–87

Ginger syrup, 302

Grapefruit

citrus and dry-cured olive salad, 163–64

-dill shrub, 307

snap pea and Asian pear salad with burrata, hazelnuts, and, 107–8

Grapes

Concord, and pomegranate molasses, 32

Fuyu persimmon salad with red walnuts, sherry vinegar, and, 186

pickled, poblano soup with pancetta and, 216–17

pickled rooibos, 24

Grits, creamy, with blistered tomatoes, pickled serrano chiles, and sunflower-miso tahini, 238–40

H

Hamachi crudo with adjika, yuzu-dashi vinaigrette, avocado, and potato croquettes, 154–56

Harissa, mortar-and-pestle, 62

Harrough, 42–44

Hazelnuts

and fennel dukkah, 48

mortar-and-pestle romesco, 60

roasted golden beets with radishes, cucumbers, creamy poblano-feta dressing, and, 218–20

snap pea and Asian pear salad with grapefruit, burrata, and, 107–8

Honey

cubeb, 33

fennel, 33

fennel pollen, 33

saffron, 33

Horseradish yogurt, 249–51

Huckleberries

pickled, 29

sweet-and-sour, 28

"Hummus"

beets bi tahina, 182

English pea and dill, 184

fava, with mint and Pecorino cheese, 227

I

Imjadra with cherries, parsley, sumac yogurt, and fried shallots, 230–32

J

Jicama salad with mango, fennel, cucumber, peanuts, and lime and fish sauce vinaigrette, 147

Juniper

-tarragon tahini dressing, creamy, 73

-tarragon vinaigrette, 72

K

Kale

fennel, shaved cauliflower, apple, and, with creamy dill dressing and bacon bread crumb persillade, 113

Tuscan, with crushed fenugreek-nigella meatballs and sherry raisins, 137–39

Kataifi, pistachio cheesecake custards with matcha sugar and, 283–86

Kochkocha, 82

Kohlrabi with crème fraîche, mint, lemon, and yuzu kosho, 128

L

Lamb

    chops, berberé double-cut, 264

    neck stew, 263

    patties, beef and, cumin-spiced, with pine nuts and raisins, 260–61

    rack, berberé, 265

    stew, tomato and, with chickpeas and curry leaf Meyer lemon pickle, 262–63

    top round, Sichuan pepper, with English pea and parsley salad, 246–48

Lebni with eggplant purée, fava "hummus," and za'atar, 228

Lengua "schnitzel" with brown butter, capers, and cherry tomatoes, 172–74

Lentils

    imjadra with cherries, parsley, sumac yogurt, and fried shallots, 230–32

Limes

    caramelized cauliflower with mint, pine nuts, yogurt, and, 132–33

    and fish sauce vinaigrette, 71

    -watermelon–white pepper yogurt drink, 298

M

Mango, jicama salad with fennel, cucumber, peanuts, lime and fish sauce vinaigrette, and, 147

Meatballs

    baked fenugreek-nigella pork and beef, 135–36

    berberé-spiced, 136

Melon

    Tuscan, and Persian cucumber salad with cacik, 110

    watermelon-lime–white pepper yogurt drink, 298

Mexican sriracha, 85

Meyer lemon pickle, curry leaf, 26

Miso

    -fenugreek dressing, Castelfranco with cheddar and, 98–99

    -sunflower tahini, 58

    -walnut bagna cauda, 56

Molasses

    pomegranate and beet, 32

    pomegranate and Concord grape, 32

Muhammara, 59

Mushrooms

    dashi concentrate, 76

    shiitake-lemongrass broth, smoked paprika beef shoulder braised with, 255–56

O

Ocean trout, slow-roasted berberé-cured, with lemon tempura and citrus and olive salad, 166–68

Oils, 17

Olives

    dry-cured, and citrus salad, 163–64

    panfried rainbow trout with brown butter, Meyer lemon, chives, and, 160–62

Onions

    cipollini-buttermilk dressing, "broken," 74

    mint and rose pickled red, 22

Orange blossom chantilly cream, 280–82

Oranges

blood, and red endive with blue cheese, dukkah, and Banyuls vinaigrette, 104–6

citrus and dry-cured olive salad, 163–64

sautéed, barley porridge with ginger and, 212–13

and soy-glazed duck, whole roasted, 267–68

P

Pancakes

bulgur, with grape leaves, raisins, and goat cheese, 193

corn, griddled, with aonori mascarpone butter, 146

Pancetta

poblano soup with pickled grapes and, 216–17

rutabaga and, with lemon, anchovy, and capers, 190–92

Panna cotta, yogurt, with pickled huckleberries, 288

Parsley

bacon bread crumb persillade, 55

chermou-lata, 68–69

chimichurri, 84

and English pea salad, Sichuan pepper lamb top round with, 246–48

mint and fines herbes salsa verde, 70

Pasta

hand-torn, 201–3

hand-torn, pork belly with sujuk spices and, 207–8

hand-torn, with yuzu, dashi, and brown butter, 204–6

pappardelle, 203

pappardelle, tomato-dill, with caraway bread crumbs, 169–70

Pastes

harrough, 42–44

mortar-and-pestle harissa, 62

muhammara, 59

Peaches

sautéed, and shishito peppers with goat cheese, cashews, and saffron honey, 221–23

-sumac shrub, 307

Peanuts

jicama salad with mango, fennel, cucumber, lime and fish sauce vinaigrette, and, 147

Virginia, and coriander dukkah, 47

Peas

English, and dill "hummus," 184

English, and parsley salad, Sichuan pepper lamb top round with, 246–48

snap, and Asian pear salad with grapefruit, burrata, and hazelnuts, 107–8

Pepitas (pumpkin seeds)

arbol-guajillo furikake, 39

Persillade, bacon bread crumb, 55

Persimmon salad, Fuyu, with grapes, red walnuts, and sherry vinegar, 186

Pickles

curry leaf Meyer lemon, 26

huckleberries, 29

red onions, mint and rose, 22

rooibos grapes, 24

serrano chiles, 238–40

Pineapple

blackberry–Thai basil fruit mash, 303

cherry-mint fruit mash, 302

strawberry-tarragon fruit mash, 303

Pine nuts

berberé-spiced meatballs, 136

chermou-lata, 68–69

cumin-spiced beef and lamb patties with raisins and, 260–61

Piquillo peppers

mortar-and-pestle harissa, 62

mortar-and-pestle romesco, 60

muhammara, 59

Pistachios

cheesecake custards with matcha sugar and kataifi, 283–86

cheesecake with matcha sugar, 286

-rosewater yogurt drink, 299

Polenta

griddled corn cake with aonori mascarpone butter, 144–46

griddled corn pancakes with aonori mascarpone butter, 146

Pomegranates

and beet molasses, 32

and Concord grape molasses, 32

Fuyu persimmon salad with grapes, red walnuts, and sherry vinegar, 186

Pork

belly with sujuk spices and hand-torn pasta, 207–8

meatballs, baked fenugreek-nigella beef and, 135–36

meatballs, berberé-spiced, 136

porchetta, bacharat-spiced, 258

Potato croquettes, 151–52

Pudding, canela rice, with salty caramel and orange blossom cream, 280–82

R

Radicchio

Castelfranco with cheddar and miso-fenugreek dressing, 98–99

Treviso, roasted Romanesco and, with yuzu and dashi, 122–24

Rainbow trout, panfried, with brown butter, Meyer lemon, green olives, and chives, 160–62

Raisins

bulgur pancakes with grape leaves, goat cheese, and, 193

chicken escabeche with mint, 252–54

cumin-spiced beef and lamb patties with pine nuts and, 260–61

Tuscan kale with crushed fenugreek-nigella meatballs and, 137–39

Rapini

flowering choy with lime and fish sauce vinaigrette, 130

Rice

creamy Pecorino, berberé chicken and, 196–98

pudding, canela, with salty caramel and orange blossom cream, 280–82

Romanesco

roasted, and Treviso radicchio with yuzu and dashi, 122–24

soup, creamy, with grapefruit, nigella, and fresh horseradish, 120

Romesco, mortar-and-pestle, 60

Rosewater-pistachio yogurt drink, 299

Rub, coffee-spice, 40

Rutabaga and pancetta with lemon, anchovy, and capers, 190–92

S

Saffron honey, 33

Salads

    cabbage slaw with crème fraîche, mitsuba, and kochkocha, 102

    "Caesar" Brussels sprouts, 125–26

    Castelfranco with cheddar and miso-fenugreek dressing, 98–99

    citrus and dry-cured olive, 163–64

    eggplant with avocado, Persian cucumbers, herbs, and cipollini-buttermilk dressing, 194–95

    English pea and parsley, Sichuan pepper lamb top round with, 246–48

    fennel, kale, shaved cauliflower, and apple with creamy dill dressing and bacon bread crumb persillade, 113

    Fuyu persimmon, with grapes, red walnuts, and sherry vinegar, 186

    jicama, with mango, fennel, cucumber, peanuts, and lime and fish sauce vinaigrette, 147

    kohlrabi with crème fraîche, mint, lemon, and yuzu kosho, 128

    red endive and blood oranges with blue cheese, dukkah, and Banyuls vinaigrette, 104–6

    salted cucumbers with avocado and ginger-soy dressing, 112

    snap pea and Asian pear, with grapefruit, burrata, and hazelnuts, 107–8

    Tuscan melon and Persian cucumber, with cacik, 110

Salbitxada, 63

Salmorejo, 66

Salsa verde, mint and fines herbes, 70

Salt, 17

Sauces. *See also* Pastes

    chermou-lata, 68–69

    chimichurri, 84

    fenugreek-chipotle tomato, 67

    kochkocha, 82

    Mexican sriracha, 85

    mint and fines herbes salsa verde, 70

    mortar-and-pestle romesco, 60

    salbitxada, 63

    salmorejo, 66

    tomato-dill, 169

Sesame seeds

    arbol-guajillo furikake, 39

    blackberry sesame cake with cardamom sugar, 293

    sunflower-miso tahini, 58

    toasting, 45

Shichimi togarashi, urfa biber, 38

Shrimp, panko-crusted, with chives and Mexican sriracha, 148–50

Shrub-and-sodas, 304–7

Shrubs

    celery, 306

    grapefruit-dill, 307

    peach-sumac, 307

Slaw, cabbage, with crème fraîche, mitsuba, and kochkocha, 102

Soups

    buttermilk-cacik, chilled, with dill and walnuts, 214

    poblano, with pancetta and pickled grapes, 216–17

    Romanesco, creamy, with grapefruit, nigella, and fresh horseradish, 120

Spice blends

    arbol-guajillo furikake, 39

    baharat, 35

    berberé, 36

    coffee-spice rub, 40

    harrough, 42–44

    urfa biber shichimi togarashi, 38

    za'atar, 17

Spigarello, orange-scented creamed, with almonds and Aleppo pepper, 224

Sriracha, Mexican, 85

Strawberries

    -elderflower fool, 274

    -tarragon fruit mash, 303

Sudachi-cucumber yogurt drink, 298

Sunflower-miso tahini, 58

Sweet potatoes with aonori mascarpone butter, feta, and honey, 188

Syrup

    ginger, 302

T

Tahini

    dressing, creamy juniper-tarragon, 73

    sunflower-miso, 58

Tangerine-mint yogurt drink, 299

Tomatoes

    blistered, creamy grits with pickled serrano chiles, sunflower-miso tahini, and, 238–40

    braised chicken with leeks, berberé, thyme, yogurt, and, 234–35

    cherry, lengua "schnitzel" with brown butter, capers, and, 172–74

    -dill pappardelle with caraway bread crumbs, 169–70

    -dill sauce, 169

    and lamb stew with chickpeas and curry leaf Meyer lemon pickle, 262–63

    Mexican sriracha, 85

    nigella-lavender albacore with ume and, 241–43

    salbitxada, 63

    salmorejo, 66

    sauce, fenugreek-chipotle, 67

U

Urfa biber shichimi togarashi, 38

V

Vinaigrettes

    adjika, 64

    juniper-tarragon, 72

    lime and fish sauce, 71

    walnut, 107–8

    yuzu-dashi, 77

W

Walnuts

    cacik, 92

    chilled buttermilk-cacik soup with dill and, 214

    Fuyu persimmon salad with grapes, sherry vinegar, and, 186

    -miso bagna cauda, 56

    muhammara, 59

    vinaigrette, 107–8

Watermelon-lime–white pepper yogurt drink, 298

Y

Yogurt. *See also* Yogurt drinks

    cacik, 92

    horseradish, 249–51

    in a jar, 90

    panna cotta with pickled huckleberries, 288

Yogurt drinks, 297

    rosewater-pistachio, 299

    sudachi-cucumber, 298

    tangerine-mint, 299

    watermelon-lime–white pepper, 298

Yu choy

    flowering choy with lime and fish sauce vinaigrette, 130

Yuzu-dashi vinaigrette, 77

Z

Za'atar, 17

ENTRANCE

JOE'S

PUBLIC
PARKING

BROADWAY SHOPS
BARS & REST